24 April 1996

Living in Harmony

Living in Harmony
Nature Writing by Women in Canada

edited and with an introduction by
Andrea Pinto Lebowitz

ORCA BOOK PUBLISHERS

Canadian Cataloguing in Publication Data
Main entry under title:
  Living in Harmony

  Includes bibiliographical references.
  ISBN 1-55143-060-6

  1. Canadian literature (English) – Women authors. 2. Nature – Literary collections. 3. Natural history – Canada – Literary collections. 4. Women – Canada – Literary collections. 1. Lebowitz, Andrea Pinto.
PS8235.W7L58 1996   C810.8'036   C95-911170-0
PR9194.5W7L58 1996

The publisher would like to acknowledge the ongoing financial support of the Canada Council, the British Columbia Ministry of Small Business, Tourism and Culture, and the Department of Canadian Heritage.

Cover design by Christine Toller
Cover painting: Landon Mackenzie, Canoe/Woman, 1988, acrylic on canvas,
     60" x 72", courtesy the private collection of Sandra Pitblado
Printed and bound in Canada

Orca Book Publishers   Orca Book Publishers
PO Box 5626, Station B   PO Box 468
Victoria, BC V8R 6S4   Custer, WA 98240-0468
Canada   USA

10 9 8 7 6 5 4 3 2 1

for Wayne, as always

Acknowledgements

I wish to thank Dr. Evan Alderson, Dean of Arts at
Simon Fraser University, for his generous support —
personal and financial; Lorelei Lingard for her
enthusiasm and encouragement as well as her research
assistance and manuscript preparation; and Wayne
Wiens for his unending patience, technical assistance
and editorial advice.

Table of Contents

Sandy Shreve   *Whale Watching*   ix
Introduction   1

Origins   9

Angela Sidney   *How the World Began*   11
Emily Pauline Johnson-Tekahionwake   from *Legends of Vancouver*   22
Emily Carr   *Beginnings*   33
Sharon Butala   *The Subtlety of Land*   37

Explorations   53

Anna Brownell Jameson   *It was very beautiful*   55
Mary T. S. Schaffer   *A Maiden Voyage on the "New" Lake*   61

Home   69

Laura Beatrice Berton   from *I Married the Klondike*   71
Theodora Stanwell-Fletcher   *A Northern Spring*   81
Chris Czajkowski   *Raising the Roof*   96

Encounters   105

Emily Carr   *Green*   107
Louise de Kiriline Lawrence   *An Exercise in Tolerance*   110
Peri McQuay   *On a Morning so Beautiful it Makes a Mockery of Fear*   126
Gilean Douglas   *Merry Christmas To All*   133

Place   139

Catharine Parr Traill   *Canadian Wild Flowers*   141
Aleta Karstad   from *Canadian Nature Notebook*   150
Mary Majka   *Waters Slow, Waters Swift*   160
Merilyn Simonds Mohr   *Stubborn Particulars of Place*   168

Gardens   175

Emily Carr   *White Currants*   177
Midge Ellis Keeble   *Birds, Bees and Other Weirds*   180
Stephanie Quainton Steel   *Salal Joe's Garden*   188

For the Future   199

Alexandra Morton   from *In the Company of Whales*   201
Severn Cullis-Suzuki   *Tell The World*   208

On the Form   213

Peri McQuay   *Seizing the Strawberry*   215

Permissions   225
Further Reading   227

Sandy Shreve

Whale Watching

from *Bewildered Rituals* (1992)

for Andrea Lebowitz

All week we search through sightings
of seals and otters
and lost logs in the water
for the orcas

Hoping to see fins in the distance
binoculars raised
we whisk our eyes across wave
after wave, wish away the constant
ferries and outboards
want the channel a calm
invitation for whales

as if our seeing them
would be a proof of possibility
that all we have inflicted
on this world
might be reversed
and all the ruin changed
to an unscathed grace

as if the common seal
no longer counts enough for this
approaches going home
with a story of sea gulls
instead of eagles

Do we want the rare, endangered
species to visit us
to bestow some special privilege
like a trust
that tells us we are not
the culprits

I want to believe it's something else
this longing for the exotic
something that transcends
such tired desires

Of course, the time comes
when we give up
accept a pattern of metallic slaps
as one more shipping sound
Engrossed in books we let it pass
until by accident of a glance
we glimpse the last three whales
breaching in the bay just yards away

We gaze, trapped between elation and regret
in that moment luck has granted —
kicking ourselves for what we missed
we still feel honoured by the orcas
who likely neither know nor care
that we are, wistful, there
wishing they'd come back
give us one more chance

Introduction

As I sit in my garden on a perfect spring day, I turn to my laptop computer to set down this introduction. The scene strikes me as an emblem of the works collected in this anthology, for nature writing links moments of appreciation of nature with scientific awareness and close observation. For these authors a sense of wonder and aesthetic delight combined with intense study leads to reflections on the ethics of our relationship to the natural world. For all the writers whose voices you will hear in this anthology, the goal is to find ways to live in harmony with nature and to act as stewards of the land — especially as the natural world grows more and more threatened. Their familiarity with the environment fosters wonder and respect and a passionate desire to convey this personal experience to the reader. Thus while grounded in natural history and scientific observation, nature writing moves us by the intensity of its details, imagery and lyric voice.

Nature has been a presence in literature from the earliest written texts, but this non-fiction prose achieved its present contour in the late eighteenth century in the work of Gilbert White. *The Natural History and Antiquities of Selborne* (1789), a collection of letters written to fellow naturalists in England, demonstrates many of the characteristics that continue to mark the form: a personal voice, keen observation of the natural world, speculation on the science that explains the observation and a fervent delight and concern for the environment. The tradition of daily encounters with the land and speculations about these meetings frequently appears in journal as well as letter form and both these types of writing continue to be employed today. A listener to CBC's "Morningside" will hear occasional contributions from Chris Czajkowski whose work *Cabin at Singing*

River, a journal of the making of a wilderness home, began as a series of letters to the "Morningside" host Peter Gzowski.

The collection is confined to the land now called Canada and to the work of women. Both of these choices were made to suggest new ways of seeing the experience of the natural world. Canadians are said to fear nature and to suffer from a "garrison mentality" that rejects nature not only for its power and danger, but more fundamentally because of its supposed obliteration of human values. This ideology of our relationship to the land, first formulated in the work of Northrop Frye, finds powerful representations in many literary works, but it is not the whole story. Alongside the tale of fear and loathing is another narrative. In this story, nature may well be dangerous and awesome, but it is also a place of beauty, solace and home. Rather than cancelling human values and aspirations, the natural world offers an alternative way of being human through harmony with the land. This second story is told in the works of this anthology which is organized into the narrative of origins and exploration, finding home, encounters and place, and finally, thoughts for the future.

The decision to select only the works of women is also a way to tell another story. Except for early settlement journals, the work of women nature writers has been hidden from history. Yet this obscuring has more to do with the perceptions of the historians than with the merits of the female writers. Bringing these women back into focus redresses a wrong of literary history but more importantly it offers another way of seeing our connection to the land. While the story of the garrison is largely a male narrative, it is clearly not shared by many men, particularly nature writers. As with their brothers, women nature writers do not concur with the garrison mentality nor do they necessarily have the same outlook as the male authors. Rather the sense of wonder and respect common to all nature writers is filtered through the experience of being a woman. These writers find new ways of living through their encounters with wilderness. At times they discover solace in isolation from conventional domestic arrangements; at other times the land offers a haven for the fulfilment of traditional relationships.

Because these are personal essays based upon individual experience, the particularities of daily life are significant and no event or part of creation is too minute to inspire attention nor too inconsequential to cause reflection. The range of topics and the emotions they inspire is as vast as the subject matter. Consequently there are many variations possible within

this form and this anthology gathers together some of the major representations of the genre written in English by women in Canada.

While these selections offer different ways of seeing, taken together
they also tell a tale. Chronology is not as meaningful as situation, place and
theme. The beginning of the anthology is in origins, in stories of how individuals and their tribes people the land. In the First Nations texts, these
stories are transcriptions of legends and myths that simultaneously tell the
beginning of nature and the beginning of people. While there is a separation between the human and natural worlds, the two are still fluid and
permeable and boundaries can be breached and mutated. Humans, if anything, are inferior rather than superior to nature. European immigrant
writers may not subscribe to this view of hierarchy, but the women among
them, as witnessed by these works, desire neither conquest nor capitula-
tion, but harmony and respect. As early as the 1830s, Catharine Parr Traill
is regretting that a particularly felicitous landscape will be devastated by
the construction of a sawmill. And while she can see the usefulness of the
mill, she questions the notion that human "progress" and "need" must be
at the expense of the natural world.

Among the first European women are travellers and explorers, but unlike their male counterparts, they do not come for economic or spiritual
conquest. Rather, these women seem driven by curiosity, a taste for danger
and discovery and a desire to escape the confines of the social roles imposed
on women. For example, Mary Schaffer, a society woman from Philadelphia,
doffed her ball gowns for riding gear and went in search not of gold or
treasure, but the wildflowers of the Rockies. While many travellers did not
remain in Canada, the natural world that they experienced here was a spiritual
and emotional home that grounded their future decisions and experiences.

Because of the progressive settlement of the country, the process of
making a home occurs over and over with each new area. Even more fundamentally, the arrival in a new place and the attempt to understand it
mark a passage into a new way of being. Sharon Butala's work *The Perfection
of the Morning: An Apprenticeship in Nature* (1994) records her marriage and
move from the city to the country, where a new life opens to her both in
her human relationships and her connection to the rural world. These
events occur in the late decades of the twentieth century, yet the initiation
and transformation she undergoes have much that is reminiscent of nine-
teenth-century settlement journals. Her story of and in the land is one of
rebirth and origins.

Making a home and learning the land are the beginnings of a new story for many of these writers. For Catharine Parr Traill, observing the natural world and making it home are synonymous. As an amateur naturalist, she studied and collected plants and animals, catalogued them and recorded her findings. Often, through letters back to England, she, like Gilbert White, wrote of her discoveries and observations and asked for assistance in identifying specimens. As her knowledge of her new home increased she was able to produce guides to the wildflowers of her area.

Catharine Parr Traill's schooling in the first part of the nineteenth century was a typical form of female education. From the eighteenth century on, young women in England were trained in botanical subjects. At first this instruction tended toward a sentimental review of the meaning of flowers and the analogies between the floral and the female, but increasingly the training became more rigorous and scientific, and the women enthusiastic naturalists. This spirit of inquiry vivifies travel diaries and journals as well as settlement narratives. Not surprisingly, some of Canada's earliest naturalists and nature writers are female. Their decline into obscurity has more to do with the vagaries of history than with the value of their work. It is my hope that this anthology will right the balance and bring back into focus the original and continuing contribution of women to understanding, documenting and reflecting on the natural history of Canada.

This, of course, raises the issue of gender and writing. Since gender is one of the fundamental ways in which we define ourselves and our role in the world, it is necessary to inquire into the impact that gender has on literary production. The question is always pertinent, but we cannot expect to get the same answer in each case. The building of a log cabin in the wilderness is an unusual story in the past or present. That Chris Czajkowski and Gilean Douglas make these homes alone raises questions about the achievement of a single woman in the wilderness. For a woman alone, the wilderness offers an alternative to conventional ideas of domesticity and relationship, and observation and interaction with animals, an important aspect of nature writing, displace human relationship.

However, the reader's attention to gender may not be the same as the writers'. Peri McQuay argues that gender is not a major determinant in her writing, while Theodora Stanwell-Fletcher frequently comments upon the way in which life in the wilderness allows her to escape and transcend gender roles and limitations. Since definitions of male and female are not innate but created by individual societies, it is not surprising that these writers see their womanhood differently and note its effects on their writing variously. The conclusion seems to be that the inquiry into gender is worthwhile as long as the reader does not expect all women nature writers to produce the same type of work. The justice of returning voice to forgotten or marginal writers is, however, without question.

While the making and finding of home in nature is a recurring goal, this may not always be connected with the creation of domesticity. As already suggested, some writers find home by eschewing personal relationships while others find home in a domestic unit. But even with the creation of a home base, the variations of the form are not exhausted. Frequently these writers observe the flora and fauna of the environment, and a writer like Louise de Kiriline Lawrence is important not only for her writing, but also for her detailed observation and recording of bird populations over a period in excess of fifty years. Similarly, Merilyn Simonds Mohr, Aleta Karstad and Mary Majka concentrate on the particularities of specific sites and help to define and celebrate a place through its botanical and animal species.

A type of work that fits ambiguously with this genre is garden writing. Obviously it can be quite diametrically opposed to nature writing in its attempt to control and transform wilderness into human landscape rather than to appreciate the natural world in and for itself. Yet the desire — and need — to garden is often part of a nature writer's life and the gardening events that happen spontaneously and with an unplanned felicity often bring garden writing into the sphere of nature writing. On the other hand nature writers record their encounters with animals and places that emphasize the gap between the human and the natural as well as offering connections that invest the writer's world with newly understood purpose and meaning.

Significance springs from study of the events and creatures of the natural world and understanding often derives from visual as well as verbal representations. The work of the illustrator and artist has always been connected to the work of the nature writer. As women were trained in botanical drawing at a time when there were no photographic means of illustrating nature, their contributions to the advance of scientific knowledge are profound if anonymous. More importantly, the attempt to illustrate offers a way of knowing that is beyond the reach of verbal description. Attending to an object with the regard necessary for illustration conveys a knowledge and connection not available through words alone. For Emily Carr, writing and

drawing were symbiotic ways to come to know and capture her understanding of the natural world, and she kept a journal of her observations in
which she tried to work out in words the meanings she was attempting in
paint. Aleta Karstad suggests that "the image teaches me so much more
than any less reconstructive methods of observation could. I have found
that to draw is to learn."

It is not, therefore, surprising that many of these writers are also artists. Emily Carr is the best known, but the work of Catharine Parr Traill as
a nature illustrator complements her botanical writing and many others
such as Aleta Karstad, Mary Schaffer, Chris Czajkowski, Alexandra Morton
and Stephanie Quainton Steele excel as visual artists as well as writers.
Interestingly, Karstad has illustrated the work of two of the other authors
in this anthology, Louise de Kiriline Lawrence and Peri McQuay. Thus even
today, despite sophisticated photographic possibilities, the hand-created
illustration can convey not only the form of the object but also the individual's
aesthetic and emotional response to the natural world, in a unique and
personal way.

This returns us to the issue of the personal voice in nature writing.
The origin of the texts are in the individuals' encounters with and concern
for nature. Because of their commitment to the land, these authors cham-
pion environmental preservation and protection. Some of them see this
responsibility as particularly related to their roles as women, but all concur
that men as well as women must nurture the land. This commitment is
apparent throughout but in the work of Alexandra Morton, the message is
directed specifically to the next generation to inherit the earth. She tries to
convey her sense of wonder at nature and to instruct her young readers in
the skills of marine biology and scientific observation. Her audience is
thus introduced to a world which may be remote from their urban lives
and invited to partake in the work of natural history. Interestingly the youngest voice in this anthology is that of Severn Cullis-Suzuki who, coincidentally,
is considering a career as a marine biologist. As a thirteen-year-old she
made an impassioned plea to the delegates to the Earth Summit on the
Environment (UNCED) held in Brazil in 1992. She challenged her elders
to protect the future for her tribe and for the earth. Filled with dread at the
loss of both futures, she charges us all to look to our responsibilities to our
children and to the earth that they will inherit.

Told as a narrative, these works record the story of women's views of
the origins, explorations and settlement of the land. Grounded in the indi-

viduals' perceptions, these essays give voice to encounters with the natural world and its creatures through attention to the particularities of places. For all these writers the desire to steward the land goes with a concern for the future. The collection concludes with an essay by Peri McQuay, who speculates on the future of the form and confronts the question: should a genre that celebrates nature continue to be pursued when the very subject is faced with mortal danger?

Origins

Angela Sidney
(1902 – 1991)

Angela Sidney described herself as a Tagish and Tlingit woman of the Deisheetaan (Crow) Clan. She was born in the southern Yukon. In 1986 she received the Order of Canada for scholarly contributions and community service. In these contemporary (late 1980s) retellings of traditional legends, Sidney recounts the beginning of the world told as a story. She narrates the events of creation as she heard them from her father in the early part of this century and adapts them to the changing reality of her world over the last sixty years. In the first section Crow creates people and animals, while a human mother produces the animals in the second part of the story. Finally the animal/humans of the third episode breach the winter sky enclosing life on earth to bring summer and growth to our world. All parts of this creation story demonstrate the interdependence of animals and humans.

How the World Began

from *Life Lived Like a Story* (1990)

"You tell what you know.
The way I tell stories is what I know."

The Story of Crow

One time there was a girl whose daddy is a very high
  man.
They kept her in her bedroom all the time —
Men tried to marry her all the time, but they say no, she's
  too good.
Crow wanted to be born — he wants to make the world!
So he made himself into a pine needle.
A slave always brings water to that girl, and one time he
  gets water with a pine needle in it.
She turns it down — makes him get fresh water.
Again he brings it. Again a pine needle is there.
Four times he brings water and each time it's there.
Finally, she just gave up — she spit that pine needle out
  and drank the water.
But it blew into her mouth and she swallowed it.
Soon that girl is pregnant.

Her mother and daddy are mad.
Her mother asks, "Who's that father?"
"No, I never know a man," she told her mother.

That baby starts to grow fast.
That girl's father had the sun, moon, stars, daylight
    hanging in his house.
He's the only one that has them.
The world was all dark, all the time.
The child begged for them to play with.

Finally, the father gives his grandchild the sun to play
    with.
He rolls it around, plays with it, laughs, has lots of fun.
Then he rolls it to the door and out it goes!

"Oh!" he cries. He just pretends.
He cries because that sun is lost.

"Give me the moon to play with."

They say no, at first — like now, if a baby asks for the sun
    or moon you say,
"That's your grandfather's fire."
Finally, they gave it to him.

One by one they gave him the sun, moon, stars, daylight —
He loses them all.

"Where does she get that child from? He loses
    everything!"
That's what her father says.

Then Crow disappears.
He has those things with him in a box.
He walks around — comes to a river.
Lots of animals there — fox, wolf, wolverine, mink, rabbit.
Everybody's fishing ...
That time animals all talk like people talk now —
The world is dark.

"Give me fish," Crow says.
No one pays any attention.
"Give me fish or I'll bring daylight!"
They laugh at him.

He's holding a box … starts to open it and lets one ray
  out.
Then they pay attention!
He opens that box a bit more — they're scared!
Finally, he opens that daylight box and threw it out.
Those animals scatter!
They hide in the bush and turn into animals like now.
Then the sun, moon, stars, and daylight come out.

"Go to the skies," Crow says.
"Now no one man owns it — it will be for everybody."

He is right, what he says, that Crow.

After Crow made the world, he saw that sea lion owned
  the only island in the world.
The rest was water — he's the only one with land.
The whole place was ocean!
Crows rests on piece of log — he's tired.
He sees sea lion with that little island just for himself.
He wants some land, too, so he stole that sea lion's kid.

"Give me back that kid!" said sea lion.

"Give me beach, some sand," says Crow.

So sea lion gave him sand.
Crow threw that sand around the world.
"Be world," he told it. And it became the world.

After that, he walks around, flies around all alone.
He's tired — he's lonely — he needs people.
He took poplar tree bark. You know how it's thick?
He carved it and then he breathed into it.

"Live!" he said, and he made a person.
He made Crow and Wolf, too.
At first they can't talk with each other —
Crow man and woman are shy with each other — look
  away.
Wolf is same way, too.

14

"This is no good," he said. So he changed that.
He made Crow man sit with Wolf woman.
And he made Wolf man sit with Crow woman.
So Crow must marry Wolf and Wolf must marry Crow.

Game Mother

This is the story of how game animals used to be.

This Game Mother, she's just an ordinary woman like us.
She got married to two young brothers. She had two
   husbands — brothers.
They stayed together I don't know how many years and
   they never have a baby.
They never travel — she doesn't want to travel around.
Just stay one place all the time.

When fall starts to come her husbands always make
   snowshoes for her.
The oldest one gets his snowshoes done first — then the
   youngest one.
She wouldn't work on it either.
Every time they finish, they wrap that snowshoe up in
   nice cloth and give it to her.

Here she always put it in back of her pillow and said to it.
"You undo yourself.'
She didn't want to travel with it.
Here in the morning, it would be all undone so next day
   they'd start another one always.
And then the youngest one made snowshoes for her ...
   same thing.
She always put it in back of her pillow:
"You undo yourself."
And in the morning it would be undone.

I don't know how many years they were like that — just
   stay in one place.
Oh, they get tired, I guess, those boys.
But she never got tired.

And here she started to grow, bigger and bigger and
    bigger like that.
And she wouldn't go anyplace, wouldn't travel around.
She was just so big.

Springtime, that's the time when animals are born.
She told her husbands,
"It's no use because I'm no good to you people.
You'd better go on your own.
Just leave me right here.
But make a better housecamp for me."
That's what she told them.

"If you want to, you can watch me from a long ways away,
From on top of the mountain."

Anyway, they left.
They hated to go, but they had to go anyway.
They watched, I guess, all the time.
I wonder what kind of fieldglasses they got, eh?

The first thing they know, moose was born.
As soon as those husbands go, those animals came out!
Moose had grizzly teeth, too, they say —
She called it back and she took those teeth out.
She showed moose what to eat — willow.
Bull moose came with a horn.
"Leave your horn once in a while," she told him.
"Don't use it all the time, just in running [rutting]
    season."
Then she told moose to lick salt in her ashes.
They call it "moose lick."

Caribou came next — first bull and then cow.
Bull caribou came with horns, too, so she told him the
    same thing.
"Leave your horns once in a while.
Don't use them all the time, just in running season.
Just then you use it," she told them.
And she taught them to eat moss.

Next sheep came, and she taught him to eat grass.

Then came grizzly — she tried to call him back to take his
    teeth out, but he wouldn't come.
She couldn't get it!
"I'm going to use these teeth to get even," he told her.
"You're taking everything from us."
"Well, don't be mean to people," she told him.
"Remember that you came from people."

After grizzly, came wolf.
And after wolf, came goat.
Everything came from her!
She gave them a meal right away, as soon as they came, to
    teach them what to eat.

Finally, rabbit came out last.
And he started eating branches off her campfire —
That's why in wintertime rabbits eat pine tree branches.

Those animals started staying around her place, just
    around her.
They don't know what she eats — what she lives on.
She stayed for one whole year.
Finally, the next year, she got tired of them.
They make too much noise, eat up everything — all the
    grass around her place.
So she made a big swing for them, a trampoline.
She called it akeyf, that's den k'e, Tagish language.
She made big sport day for them because she's going to
    leave them.
Falltime, she made it from bull moose skin.
There's no moose before that! Where she got that, I
    don't know!
Anyway, that's the story — it was bull moose skin.
She put it up right in the middle of Bennett Lake.
It had four strings:
One went to Grey Mountain, Takaadi T'ooch' — that
    means "Charcoal mountain" in Tlingit.

One went to the mountain behind Chooutla school,
    Métaatl'e Shéch'ee:
That means "wind on the forehead" in Tagish language.
One went to Fourth of July Mountain: Médzih Dzéle' —
    that means "caribou mountain" —
And one went to that mountain we call Chílíh Dzéle' —
    "gopher mountain."

They walked out on that line that ties the swing.
The first one to come is moose — even that narrow, they
    walk on it!

Bull moose sings his song first:
"What is this they put out for me?
I'm walking on it, look at me."

They say he stepped through the skin he's so heavy.
Then the cow comes — then the calf — each one has its
    song.
That calf can hardly stand up!

Then the caribou came with its young one —
By that time, they had young ones.
Then came sheep — all that were born, they sat on the
    swing.
Then wolf came and sang his song.
Then came the rabbit song. He says,
"My brothers always do that for me.
They chop down trees and give me food
And I always play around with it."

After she got through with that skin,
She told them she's going to part with them now.
"You go all into different countries.
Go!" she said.

Somebody was watching all this from way back there.
His name is Tudech'ade —
That means "duck head feathers" in Tagish language.
He saw when she parted with them.

She didn't go very far —
Right to that Chílíh Dzéle' at Carcross.
She camped there — that's where she slept.
They call it "grizzly bear mother's camp" — Xúts Tláa
      Ta.eetí.

Next day, she went to another mountain.
On top of the mountain, you see there's two big dips.
At the first camp she wasn't comfortable in that bed.
So she moved a little way from there to that Lanning Mountain,
Kwakah Dzéle'.

From there she went to Teslin — Three Aces, they call that
      mountain.
Right there they said there's a little bridge leads to a little
      mountain.
At that mountain they say there's a dip there, too —
Green grass grows around it.

From there, I don't know …
That's as far as I remember.
My father died in 1920, but he told me all these stories
      before that.

How Animals Broke through the Sky

One time the sky used to come right down to salt water.
Here the animals lived on the winter side. It was cold!
Squirrel always came amongst the other animals, crying
all the time.

One time they asked her,
"What are you crying for?"

"My kids all froze up again."
Every now and then her children, her babies, all froze up.

So they went to a meeting, all the animals: they are going
      to try to poke a hole through the sky.
They are on the winter side and they are going to poke a

19

hole through the sky so they can have summertime, too.
Summer is on the other side.
So they gathered together with all kinds of people — they're
    animals, though —
Bloodsucker is the one they picked to go through that
    hole.
He poked that hole and then different animals went
    through.
Wolverine is the one who made that hole bigger —

He went through pulling a dry moose skin — made that
    hole bigger.
That's how they all got through.

Now they are going to steal good weather.
They went to a high person — he's got all the weather —
    the hot air, cold air,
He's got flowers and leaves.
So they took all that — they stole it when people weren't
    home.
But there was one old man there.
He went outside — took his blanket outside and waved it
    around his head.

"Get wintertime over there and summer over here.
Don't go away for good," he told them.
He kept them from taking summer completely away.
That's how, when winter goes for good that's the time we
    get summer.
Then when summer goes back to the south side, that's
    the time we get winter.

He waved his blanket and said,
"Don't go away for good," he told the weather.
"Go back and forth."

Those two worlds were side by side — winter on one side,
    summer on the other.
On one side were winter animals — on the other, summer
    animals.

They broke the sky down, and after, it went up.
After they got it across, they bust it — the summer bag.
Pretty soon, snow melted — they got leaves,
They had all the leaves tied up in a balloon.
Then they bust the balloon and all the summer things
    came out.

Emily Pauline Johnson-Tekahionwake
(1862 – 1913)

A woman of Mohawk lineage, Emily Pauline Johnson was born on the Six Nations Indian Reserve near Brantford, Ontario. In 1909 she moved to Vancouver, where she collected and recorded the legends of Vancouver. Acting as both ethnographer and participant, Johnson learned and recorded the narratives with the aid of Chief Joseph Capilano. Although not of Chief Capilano's tribe, she is told the stories as someone who will understand because of shared cultural values. Both of these legends emphasize the bonds between mothers and daughters and between women and the land.

The Lost Salmon-Run

from *Legends of Vancouver* (1911)

Great had been the "run," and the sockeye season was almost over. For that reason I wondered many times why my old friend, the klootchman, had failed to make one of the fishing fleet. She was an indefatigable work-woman, rivalling her husband as an expert catcher, and all the year through she talked of little else but the coming run. But this especial season she had not appeared amongst her fellow-kind. The fleet and the canneries knew nothing of her, and when I enquired of her tribes-people they would reply without explanation, "She not here this year."

But one russet September afternoon I found her. I had idled down the trail from the swans' basin in Stanley Park to the rim that skirts the Narrows, and I saw her graceful, high-bowed canoe heading for the beach that is the favourite landing-place of the "tillicums" from the Mission. Her canoe looked like a dream-craft, for the water was very still, and everywhere a blue film hung like a fragrant veil, for the peat on Lulu Island had been smouldering for days and its pungent odours and blue-grey haze made a dream-world of sea and shore and sky.

I hurried up-shore, hailing her in the Chinook, and as she caught my voice she lifted her paddle directly above her head in the Indian signal of greeting.

As she beached, I greeted her with extended eager hands to assist her ashore, for the klootchman is getting to be an old woman; albeit she paddles against tide-water like a boy in his teens.

"No," she said, as I begged her to come ashore. "I will wait — me. I just come to fetch Maarda; she been city; she come soon — now." But she left her "working" attitude and curled like a school-girl in the bow of the

23

canoe, her elbows resting on her paddle which she had flung across the gunwales.

"I have missed you, klootchman; you have not been to see me for three moons, and you have not fished or been at the canneries," I remarked.

"No," she said. "I stay home this year." Then, leaning towards me with grave import in her manner, her eyes, her voice, she added, "I have a grandchild, born first week July, so — I stay."

So this explained her absence. I, of course, offered congratulations and enquired all about the great event, for this was her first grandchild, and the little person was of importance.

"And are you going to make a fisherman of him?" I asked.

"No, no, not boy-child, it is girl-child," she answered with some indescribable trick of expression that led me to know she preferred it so.

"You are pleased it is a girl?" I questioned in surprise.

"Very pleased," she replied emphatically. "Very good luck to have girl for first grand-child. Our tribe not like yours; we want girl-children first; we not always wish boy-child born just for fights. Your people, they care only for war-path; our tribe more peaceful. Very good sign first grandchild to be girl. I tell you why: girl-child may some time be mother herself; very grand thing to be mother."

I felt I had caught the secret of her meaning. She was rejoicing that this little one should some time become one of the mothers of her race. We chatted over it a little longer and she gave me several playful "digs" about my own tribe thinking much less of motherhood than hers, and so much more of battle and bloodshed. Then we drifted into talk of the sockeye and of the hyiu chickimin the Indians would get.

"Yes, hyiu chickimin," she repeated with a sigh of satisfaction. "Always; and hyiu muck-a-muck when big salmon run. No more ever come that bad year when not any fish."

"When was that?" I asked.

"Before you born, or I, or" — pointing across the park to the distant city of Vancouver that breathed its wealth and beauty across the September afternoon — "before that place born, before white man came here — oh! long before."

Dear old klootchman! I knew by the dusk in her eyes that she was back in her Land of Legends, and that soon I would be the richer in my hoard of Indian lore. She sat, still leaning on her paddle; her eyes, half closed, rested on the distant outline of the blurred heights across the Inlet. I shall not further attempt her broken English, for this is but the shadow of her story, and without her unique personality the legend is as a flower that lacks both colour and fragrance. She called it "The Lost Salmon-Run."

"The wife of the Great Tyee was but a wisp of a girl, but all the world was young in those days; even the Fraser River was young and small, not the mighty water it is to-day; but the pink salmon crowded its throat just as they do now, and the tillicums, caught and salted and smoked the fish just as they have done this year, just as they will always do. But it was yet winter, and the rains were slanting and fogs drifting, when the wife of the Great Tyee stood before him and said:

"'Before the salmon-run I shall give to you a great gift. Will you honour me most if it is the gift of a boy-child or a girl-child?' The Great Tyee loved the woman. He was stern with her people, hard with his tribe; he ruled his council-fires with a will of stone. His medicine-man said he had no human heart in his body; his warriors said he had not human blood in his veins. But he clasped this woman's hands, and his eyes, his lips, his voice, were gentle as her own, as he replied:

"'Give to me a girl-child — a little girl-child — that she may grow to be like you, and, in turn, give to her husband children.'

"But when the tribes-people heard of his choice they arose in great anger. They surrounded him in a deep, indignant circle. 'You are a slave to the woman,' they declared, 'and now you desire to make yourself a slave to a woman-baby. We want an heir — a man-child to be our Great Tyee in years to come. When you are old and weary of tribal affairs, when you sit wrapped in your blanket in the hot summer sunshine, because your blood is old and thin, what can a girl-child do, to help either you or us? Who, then, will be our Great Tyee?'

"He stood in the centre of the menacing circle, his arms folded, his chin raised, his eyes as hard as flint. His voice, cold as stone, replied:

"'Perhaps she will give you such a man-child, and, if so, the child is yours; he will belong to you, not to me; he will become the possession of the people. But if the child is a girl she will belong to me — she will be mine. You cannot take her from me as you took me from my mother's side and forced me to forget my aged father in my service to the tribe; she will belong to me, will be the mother of my grandchildren, and her husband will be my son.'

"'You do not care for the good of your tribe. You care only for your own wishes and desires,' they rebelled. 'Suppose the salmon-run is small, we will have no food; suppose there is no man-child, we will have not Great Tyee to show us how to get food from other tribes, and we shall starve.'

"'Your hearts are black and bloodless,' thundered the Great Tyee, turning upon them fiercely, 'and your eyes are blinded. Do you wish the tribe to forget how great is the importance of a child that will some day be a mother herself, and give to your children and grandchildren a great Tyee? Are the people to live, to thrive, to increase, to become more powerful with no mother-women to bear future sons and daughters? Your minds are dead, your brains are chilled. Still, even in your ignorance, you are my people: you and your wishes must be considered. I call together the great medicine-men, the men of witchcraft, the men of magic. They shall decide the laws which will follow the bearing of either boy or girl-child. What say you, oh! mighty men?'

"Messengers were then sent up and down the coast, sent far up the Fraser River, and to the valley lands inland for many leagues, gathering as they journeyed, all the men of magic that could be found. Never were so many medicine-men in council before. They built fires and danced and chanted for many days. They spoke with the gods of the mountains, with the gods of the sea; then 'the power' of decision came to them. They were inspired with a choice to lay before the tribes-people, and the most ancient medicine-man in all the coast region arose and spoke their resolution:

"'The people of the tribe cannot be allowed to have all things. They want a boy-child and they want a great salmon-run also. They cannot have both. The Sagalie Tyee has revealed to us, the great men of magic, that both these things will make the people arrogant and selfish. They must choose between the two.'

"'Choose, oh! you ignorant tribes-people,' commanded the Great Tyee. 'The wise men of our coast have said that the girl-child who will some day bear children of her own will also bring abundance of salmon at her birth; but the boy-child brings to you but himself.'

"'Let the salmon go,' shouted the people, 'but give us a future Great Tyee. Give us the boy-child.'

"And when the child was born it was a boy.

"'Evil will fall upon you,' wailed the Great Tyee. 'You have despised a mother-woman. You will suffer evil and starvation and hunger and poverty, oh! foolish tribes-people. Did you not know how great a girl-child is?'

"That spring, people from a score of tribes came up to the Fraser for the salmon-run. They came great distances — from the mountains, the lakes, the far-off dry lands, but not one fish entered the vast rivers of the Pacific Coast. The people had made their choice. They had forgotten the honour that a mother-child would have brought them. They were bereft of their food. They were stricken with poverty. Through the long winter that followed they endured hunger and starvation. Since then our tribe has always welcomed girl-children — we want no more lost runs."

The klootchman lifted her arms from her paddle as she concluded; her eyes left the irregular outline of the violet mountains. She had come back to this year of grace — her Legend Land had vanished.

"So," she added, "you see now, maybe, why I am glad my grandchild is a girl; it means big salmon-run next year."

"It is a beautiful story, klootchman," I said, "and I feel a cruel delight that your men of magic punished the people for their ill choice."

"That because you girl-child yourself," she laughed.

There was the slightest whisper of a step behind me. I turned to find Maarda almost at my elbow. The rising tide was unbeaching the canoe, and as Maarda stepped in and the klootchman slipped astern, it drifted afloat.

"Kla-how-ya," nodded the klootchman as she dipped her paddle-blade in exquisite silence.

"Kla-how-ya," smiled Maarda.

"Kla-how-ya, tillicums," I replied, and watched for many moments as they slipped away into the blurred distance, until the canoe merged into the violet and grey of the farther shore.

The Grey Archway

The steamer, like a huge shuttle, wove in and out among the countless small islands; its long trailing scarf of grey smoke hung heavily along the uncertain shores, casting a shadow over the pearly waters of the Pacific, which swung lazily from rock to rock in indescribable beauty.

After dinner I wandered astern with the traveller's ever-present hope of seeing the beauties of a typical Northern sunset, and by some happy chance I placed my deck-stool near an old tillicum, who was leaning on the rail, his pipe between his thin, curved lips, his brown hands clasped idly, his sombre eyes looking far out to sea, as though they searched for the future — or was it that they were seeing the past?

"Kla-how-ya, tillicum!" I greeted.

He glanced round, and half smiled.

"Kla-how-ya, tillicum!" he replied, with the warmth of friendliness I have always met among the Pacific tribes.

I drew my deck-stool nearer to him, and he acknowledged the action with another half smile, but did not stir from his entrenchment, remaining as if hedging about with an inviolable fortress of exclusiveness. Yet I knew that my Chinook salutation would be a drawbridge by which I might hope to cross the moat into his castle of silence.

Indian-like, he took his time before continuing the acquaintance. Then he began in most excellent English:

"You do not know these northern waters?"

I shook my head.

After many moments he leaned forward, looking along the curve of the deck, up the channels and narrows we were threading, to a broad strip of waters off the port bow. Then he pointed with that peculiar, thoroughly Indian gesture of the palm uppermost.

"Do you see it — over there? The small island? It rests on the edge of the water, like a grey gull."

It took my unaccustomed eyes some moments to discern it; then all at once I caught its outline, veiled in the mists of distance — grey, cobwebby, dreamy.

"Yes," I replied, "I see it now. You will tell me of it — tillicum?"

He gave a swift glance at my dark skin, then nodded. "You are one of us," he said, with evidently no thought of a possible contradiction. "And you will understand, or I should not tell you. You will not smile at the story, for you are one of us."

"I am one of you, and I shall understand," I answered.

It was a full half-hour before we neared the island, yet neither of us spoke during that time; then, as the "grey gull" shaped itself into rock and tree and crag, I noticed in the very centre a stupendous pile of stone lifting itself skyward, without fissure or cleft; but a peculiar haziness about the base made me peer narrowly to catch the perfect outline.

"It is the 'Grey Archway,' " he explained simply.

Only then did I grasp the singular formation before us: the rock was a perfect archway, through which we could see the placid Pacific shimmering in the growing colours of the coming sunset at the opposite rim of the island.

"What a remarkable whim of Nature!" I exclaimed, but his brown hand was laid in a contradictory grasp on my arm, and he snatched up my comment almost with impatience.

"No, it was not Nature," he said. "That is the reason I say you will understand — you are one of us — you will know what I tell you is true. The Great Tyee did not make that archway, it was — " here his voice lowered — "it was magic, red man's medicine and magic — you savvy?"

"Long time ago," he began, stumbling into a half-broken English language, because, I think, of the atmosphere and environment, "long before you were born, or your father, or grandfather, or even his father, this strange thing happened. It is a story for women to hear, to remember. Women are the future mothers of the tribe, and we of the Pacific Coast hold such in high regard, in great reverence. The women who are mothers — o-ho! — they are the important ones, we say. Warriors, fighters, brave men, fearless daughters, owe their qualities to these mothers — eh, is it not always so?"

I nodded silently. The island was swinging nearer to us, the "Grey Archway" loomed almost above us, the mysticism crowded close, it enveloped me, caressed me, appealed to me.

"And?" I hinted.

"And," he proceeded, "this 'Grey Archway' is a story of mothers, of magic, of witchcraft, of warriors, of — love."

An Indian rarely uses the word "love," and when he does it expresses every quality, every attribute, every intensity, emotion, and passion embraced in those four little letters. Surely this was an exceptional story I was to hear.

I did not answer, only looked across the pulsing waters towards the "Grey Archway," which the sinking sun was touching with soft pastels, tints one could give no name to, beauties impossible to describe.

"You have not heard of Yaada?" he questioned. Then, fortunately, he continued without waiting for a reply. He well knew that I had never heard of Yaada, so why not begin without preliminary to tell me of her? — so ...

"Yaada was the loveliest daughter of the Haida tribe. Young braves from all the islands, from the mainland, from the upper Skeena country, came, hoping to carry her to their far-off lodges, but they always returned alone, She was the most desired of all the island maidens, beautiful, brave, modest, the daughter of her own mother.

"But there was a great man, a very great man — a medicine-man, skilful, powerful, influential, old, deplorably old, and very, very, rich; he

29

said, 'Yaada shall be my wife.' And there was a young fisherman, hand-some, loyal, boyish, poor, oh! very poor, and gloriously young, and he, too, said, 'Yaada shall be my wife.'

"But Yaada's mother sat apart and thought and dreamed, as mothers will. She said to herself, 'The great medicine-man has power, has vast riches, and wonderful magic, why not give her to him? But Ulka has the boy's heart, the boy's beauty; he is very brave, very strong; why not give her to him?'

"But the laws of the great Haida tribe prevailed. Its wise men said, 'Give the girl to the greatest man, give her to the most powerful, the rich-est. The man of magic must have his choice.'

"But at this the mother's heart grew as wax in the summer sunshine — it is a strange quality that mother's hearts are made of! 'Give her to the best man — the man her heart holds highest,' said the Haida mother.

"Then Yaada spoke: 'I am the daughter of my tribe; I would judge of men by their excellence. He who proves most worthy I shall marry; it is not riches that make a good husband; it is not beauty that makes a good father for one's children. Let me and my tribe see some proof of the excel-lence of these two men — then, only, shall I choose who is to be the father of my children. Let us have a trial of their skill; let them show me how evil or how beautiful is the inside of the hearts. Let each of them throw a stone with some intent, some purpose in their hearts. He who makes the noblest mark may call me wife.'

"'Alas! Alas!' wailed the Haida mother. 'This casting of stones does not show worth. It but shows prowess.'

"But I have implored the Sagalie Tyee of my father, and of his fathers before him, to help me to judge between them by this means,' said the girl. 'So they must cast the stones. In this way only shall I see their innermost hearts.'

"The medicine-man never looked so old as at that moment; so hope-lessly old, so wrinkled, so palsied: he was no mate for Yaada. Ulka never looked so god-like in his young beauty, so gloriously young, so courageous, The girl, looking at him, loved him — almost was she placing her hand in his, but the spirit of her forefathers halted her. She had spoken the word — she must abide by it. 'Throw!' she commanded.

"Into his shrivelled fingers the great medicine-man took a small, round stone, chanting strange words of magic all the while; his greedy eyes were on the girl, his greedy thoughts about her.

"Into his strong young fingers Ulka took a smooth, flat stone; his handsome eyes were lowered in boyish modesty, his thoughts were worshipping her. The great medicine-man cast his missile first; it swept through the air like a shaft of lightning, striking the great rock with a force that shattered it. At the touch of that stone the 'Grey Archway' opened and has remained open to this day.

"'Oh, wonderful power and magic!' clamoured the entire tribe. 'The very rocks do his bidding.'

"But Yaada stood with eyes that burned in agony. Ulka could never command such magic — she knew it. But at her side Ulka was standing erect, tall, slender, and beautiful, but just as he cast his missile the evil voice of the old medicine-man began a still more evil incantation. He fixed his poisonous eyes on the younger man, eyes with hideous magic in their depths — ill-omened and enchanted with 'bad medicine.' The stone left Ulka's fingers; for a second time it flew forth in a straight line, then as the evil voice of old man grew louder in its incantations, the stone curved. Magic had waylaid the strong arm of the young brave. The stone poised in an instant above the forehead of Yaada's mother, then dropped with the weight of many mountains, and the last long sleep fell upon her.

"'Slayer of my mother!' stormed the girl, her suffering eyes fixed upon the medicine-man. "Oh, I now see your black heart through your black magic. Through the good magic you cut the Grey Archway, but your evil magic you used upon young Ulka. I saw your wicked eyes upon him; I heard your wicked incantations; I know your wicked heart. You used your heartless magic in hope of winning me — in hope of making him an outcast of the tribe. You cared not for my sorrowing heart, my motherless life to come.' Then, turning to the tribe, she demanded: "Who of you saw his evil eyes fixed on Ulka? Who of you heard his evil song?'

"'I,' and 'I,' and 'I,' came voice after voice.

"'The air is poisoned that we breathe about him,' they shouted. 'The young man is blameless, his heart is as the sun; but the man who has used his evil magic has a heart black and cold as the hours before the dawn.'

"Then Yaada's voice arose in a strange, sweet, sorrowful chant:

My feet shall walk no more upon this island,
With its great, Grey Archway.
My mother sleeps for ever on this island,
With its great, Grey Archway.
My heart would break without her on this island,

With its great, Grey Archway.
My life was of her life upon this island,
With its great, Grey Archway.
My mother's soul has wandered from this island,
With its great, Grey Archway.
My feet must follow hers beyond this island,
With its great, Grey Archway.

"As Yaada chanted and wailed her farewell she moved slowly towards the edge of the cliff. On its brink she hovered a moment with outstretched arms, as a sea-gull poises on its weight — then she called:

"'Ulka, my Ulka! Your hand is innocent of wrong; it was the evil magic of your rival that slew my mother. I must go to her; even you cannot keep me here; will you stay, or come with me? Oh! my Ulka!'

"The slender, gloriously young boy sprang towards her; their hands closed one within the other; for a second they poised on the brink of the rocks, radiant as stars; then together they plunged into the sea."

The legend was ended. Long ago we had passed the island with its "Grey Archway"; it was melting into the twilight, far astern.

As I brooded over this strange tale of a daughter's devotion I watched the sea and sky for something that would give me a clue to the inevitable sequel that the tillicum, like all his race, was surely withholding until the opportune moment.

Something flashed though [sic] the darkening waters not a stone's-throw from the steamer. I leaned forward, watching it intently. Two silvery fish were making a succession of little leaps and plunges along the surface of the sea, their bodies catching the last tints of sunset, like flashing jewels. I looked at the tillicum quickly. He was watching me — a world of anxiety in his half-mournful eyes.

"And those two silvery fish?" I questioned.

He smiled. The anxious look vanished. "I was right," he said; "you do know us and our ways, for you are one of us. Yes, those fish are seen only in these waters; there are never but two of them. They are Yaada and her mate, seeking for the soul of the Haida woman — her mother."

Emily Carr
(1871 – 1945)

*Emily Carr is well known as one of Canada's most famous
painters whose work meditates on the nature of Canada's west coast.
As well, she produced five books of stories and reminiscences, two of
which,* The Book of Small *(1942) and* Growing Pains *(1946),
are represented in this anthology. Although Carr always kept journals,
these books were written later in her life when poor health curtailed
her painting. In the books, all of which are autobiographical, she
recounts events charged with the heightened light of memory. The
connection between nature and remembrance is an important one, for
often the environment serves as a catalyst to recollecting and
recapturing the past.* The Book of Small *concerns earliest events and
is so named because, as the youngest child but one in the family, Carr
was known as "Small."*

Beginnings

from *The Book of Small* (1942)

Victoria, on Vancouver Island, British Columbia, was the little town; I was the little girl.

It is hard to remember just when you first became aware of being alive. It is like looking through rain onto a bald, new lawn; as you watch, the brown is all pricked with pale green. You did not see the points pierce, did not hear the stab — there they are!

My father did not come straight from England to Victoria when, a lad of nineteen, he started out to see something of the world. He went to many countries, looking, thinking, choosing. At last he heard of the California gold rush and went there. He decided that California was a very fine country, but after the rush was over he went back to England, married an English girl and brought his bride out to California in a sailing ship, all round Cape Horn. Intending to settle in California, he went into business but after a while it irked Father to live under any flag other than his own. In a few years, having decided to go back "home" to live, he chartered a vessel and took to England the first shipment of California wheat. But, staunch Englishman though my Father was, the New Land had said something to him and he chafed at the limitations of the Old which, while he was away from it, had appeared perfect. His spirit grew restless and, selling all his effects, he brought his wife and two small daughters out to the new world. Round the Horn they came again, and up, up, up the west coast of America till they came to the most English-tasting bit of all Canada — Victoria on the south end of Vancouver Island, which was then a Crown Colony.

Father stood still, torn by his loyalty to the Old Land and his delight in the New. He saw that nearly all the people in Victoria were English and smiled at how they tried to be more English than the English themselves, just to prove to themselves and the world how loyal they were being to the Old Land.

Father set his family down in British Columbia. He and Mother had accepted Canada long before I, the youngest but one of their nine children, was born. By that time their homesickness was healed. Instead of being English they had broadened out into being British, just as Fort Camosun had swelled herself from being a little Hudson's Bay Fort, inside a stockade with bastions at the corners, into being the little town of Victoria, and the capital of British Columbia.

Father bought ten acres of land — part of what was known as Beckley Farm. It was over James' Bay and I have heard my mother tell how she cried at the lonesomeness of going to live in a forest. Yet Father's land was only one mile out of the town. There was but one other house near — that of Mr. James Bissett of the Hudson's Bay Company. Mr. Bissett had a wife and family. They moved East long before I was born but I was to know, when nearly grown up, what the love of those pioneer women must have been for one another, for when years later I stood at Mrs. Bissett's door in Lachine, seeing her for the first time, and said, "Mrs. Bissett, I am Emily Carr's daughter, Emily," she took me to herself in the most terrific hug.

As far back as I can remember Father's place was all made and in order. The house was large and well-built, of California redwood, the garden prim and carefully tended. Everything about it was extremely English. It was as though Father had buried a tremendous homesickness in this new soil and it had rooted and sprung up English. There were hawthorn hedges, primrose banks, and cow pastures with shrubberies.

We had an orchard and a great tin-lined apple room, wonderful strawberry beds and raspberry and currant bushes, all from imported English stock, and an Isabella grape vine which Father took great pride in. We had chickens and cows and a pig, a grand vegetable garden — almost everything we ate grew on our own place.

Just one of Father's fields was left Canadian. It was a piece of land which he bought later when Canada had made Father and Mother love her, and at the end of fifty years we still called that piece of ground "the new field." The New Field had a snake fence around it, that is, a zigzag fence made of split cedar logs or of young sapling trees laid criss-cross, their own weight holding them in place so that they required no nails. Snake fences were extravagant in land and in wood, but wood and land were cheaper in Canada in early days than were nails and hinges. You made a gate wherever you wanted one by lowering bars to pass through and piling them up again. The only English thing in our new field was a stile built across the snake fence.

The New Field was full of tall fir trees with a few oaks. The underbrush had been cleared away and the ground was carpeted with our wild Canadian lilies, the most delicately lovely of all flowers — white with bent necks and brown eyes looking back into the earth. Their long, slender petals, rolled back from their drooping faces, pointed straight up at the sky, like millions of quivering white fingers. The leaves of the lilies were very shiny-green, mottled with brown, and their perfume like heaven and earth mixed.

Sharon Butala
(1940 –)

Award-winning Sharon Butala is a well-known Canadian writer who has published several novels and short stories. The Perfection of the Morning *is her first major non-fiction work. In it she records her personal search through memory, dream and vision for the wellspring of creativity. In 1976 she married and left the urban university world of Saskatoon for the remote rural world of Eastend, Saskatchewan, in the southwest corner of the province, just north of the Montana border.* The Perfection of the Morning *explores her introduction into this rural world and meditates on the way in which nature becomes a guiding force for her life and work and an introduction into a new way of knowing. The work was nominated for the Governor General's Award in 1994.*

The Subtlety of Land

from *The Perfection of the Morning* (1994)

Some years later, when I was an established author, I said to a Toronto reporter who had asked me a question about him, "My husband is a true rural man."

"What does that mean?" the reporter asked, his voice full of skepticism.

"It means," I said, "that he understands the world in terms of wild things." I was a little surprised myself at my answer, having been called upon to explain something that until that moment had seemed self-evident, and realizing that, caught off guard, I had hit on the heart of the matter.

The reporter's pencil stopped moving, his eyes shifted away from me, he reflected, his eyes shifted back to me, and without writing anything down he changed the subject. When I told this story to a writer-naturalist friend, he said, laughing, that for the reporter my answer "does not compute."

A true rural person must be somebody born and raised on the land, outside of towns, and far from most other people. That being a given, then it follows that such life experience must result in an intrinsic understanding of the world different from that of someone raised in the cement, asphalt, glass and crowds of the city. Peter's thinking about the world was different from mine in ways that went beyond our different sexes or our different lifestyles. Where I had been trained to understand human nature from Freud and pop psychology, and the functioning of the world from classes in political economy and in history, that is, from formal education, Peter's starting point was what he had all his life lived in the midst of — it was Nature.

As years on the ranch passed, though, I began to learn from Nature too; I began to catch a glimpse of the world as he saw it through my own life in Nature. When that began to happen, a new understanding slowly, very slowly, began to dawn on me about what a life in Nature teaches one.

38

I began to see that there might be more at the root of this difference in understanding of how the world works than I had guessed at, thinking it had to do only with simple, surface matters, like understanding cattle behaviour well enough to predict their next move, or knowing the habits of antelope, or reading the sky with accuracy. I didn't yet have any idea what this deeper knowledge might be, but I watched Peter closely and tried to see what he saw.

While he was doing the spring irrigation at the hay farm, he would sometimes come across fawns only a few days old lying in the hay where they'd been left by their mothers who had gone off to forage. More than once he came to the house to get me so I could see the little spotted creature for myself. "Watch," he would say. "When they're this young they don't even move when you come near them." Then he would bend down, pick up the trusting fawn in his arms, carry it to the closest grass-covered dike, and place it gently down where the irrigation water couldn't reach it. I worried about the mother locating her baby, but he said, with the confidence born of experience, "Don't worry. It won't take her a minute to find him." When we went back hours later the fawn would always be gone. These and other incidents reminded me over and over again that Peter, and other rural people who knew no other landscape, had formed his attitude to the prairie and his understanding of its weather, its growth patterns and its animals by a lifetime of immersion in it.

In my reading and occasionally in conversation with urban visitors, I read or hear people either saying directly or implying indirectly that true rural people don't notice or appreciate the beauty in which they live. Although I don't say so, the arrogance and ignorance of such remarks always makes me angry, implying as it does that rural people lack humanity, are somehow an inferior branch of the human species, that beauty is beyond their ken. It is one thing to come from the city and be overwhelmed by the beauty of Nature and to speak of it, and another thing entirely to have lived in it so long that it has seeped into your bones and your blood and is inseparable from your own being, so that it is part of you and requires no mention or hymns of praise.

Peter preferred to do our annual spring and fall cattle drives on horseback, a trek which took three days. Bringing the cattle down to the valley around Christmastime could be very unpleasant and then it was often hard to get help, so that we sometimes made that move with only Peter, me and one other person. But three days out on the prairie during a warm spring were paradise; we never had any trouble rounding up enough riders then. If the spring move was usually a joy, the best part of it was the eight to ten miles of unbroken prairie without even any true roads through it that we used to cross each time.

I knew the first time Peter took me across those miles of prairie that I loved to be there far from towns or even houses, on native shortgrass that had never been broken, where the grass hadn't been overgrazed and was full of birds' nests in the spring, and long-eared jackrabbits as big as small dogs, antelope in the distance, and coyotes that often followed us singing all the way.

Of course, unless she's a dyed-in-the-wool, bona fide horse-and-cattlewoman herself, when it's time to move cattle, and especially if there are adolescent sons on the place, the rancher's wife usually gets stuck driving the truck. The rancher is the one with the understanding of the cattle, knowledge of the route, and the cattle-management skills. As boss and owner, he has to ride. If there are adolescents along, it's taken for granted that they'll ride because they have to learn, which has a high priority on Saskatchewan ranches, and because it's so much fun and nobody wants to deprive kids of a little harmless fun.

The rancher's wife packs the meals, stows them in the truck, serves them when the time comes and packs up after. She carries drinking water and coffee and the extra jackets or the ones taken off when the day gets too warm. She carries tack, fencing pliers and other tools, and sometimes, if the move is just before calving begins, she'll have a newborn in the back of the truck and often several of them, each one marked in some way — maybe a coloured string around its neck — so it can be returned to the right mother every few hours. As the drive wears on, she's likely to have exhausted adolescents in the cab with her, while their horses are either driven ahead or led by one of the men from his own horse. Usually, at some point, somebody will take pity on her and spell her off for an hour or so, so that she can get out into the fresh air and ride a little herself.

When you move cattle you move, depending on the weather, at the leisurely pace of about two miles an hour. For long stretches you don't need to speak at all, and you can ride a mile or more away from any other rider if you want to. As you ride, the prairie slowly seeps into you. I have never felt such pure, unadulterated joy in simple existence as I have felt at moments out on the prairie during the spring move.

Ordinarily I wouldn't get to ride until we were close to the ranch and our helpers went home. Then Peter and I changed our headquarters from the hay farm to the ranch house and we'd ride horses out to the cattle to bring them the rest of the way home. Occasionally, he'd have someone along who didn't ride and who would drive the truck so that I could ride. Most of the time, though, I reluctantly drove the truck and kept my fingers crossed for a chance either to ride, or, as I sometimes did, to walk leading Peter's horse — for me to ride him was unthinkable, the very thought making my stomach turn over and my knees quake — while Peter spelled me off in the driver's seat.

Nowadays we calve at the hay farm instead of at the ranch, mostly because it's easier to keep an eye on the cows, but also because there's shelter for them here during the inevitable calf-killing spring storms. Often, too, in spring there is no water in the ditches or fields along the way, and, of course, the cattle must have water each day, moving or not. If we calve at the hay farm — Peter not being a believer in early calving — by the time we're ready to move in late April most of the farmers along the route have seeded their crops. The traditional mistrust between farmers and ranchers being what it is, it would be dangerous if one cow strayed one foot from the road allowances, those which, usually without bothering to get permission from the municipality, farmers haven't plowed up and seeded to wheat. And cows being what they are, you never know when one might take it into her head to head out, calf at her side, racing for Alaska or Mexico across a newly seeded field with a couple of cowboys in hot pursuit. Guns have been pointed on such occasions. Nowadays, it hardly seems worth the risk.

During one of the last spring moves we made, Peter had had more people along than he'd expected and before we'd gone very far he'd given one of the kids my horse, which he'd been leading, to ride. Not long after that, he'd put my saddle — the only one with stirrups that could be shortened enough for small people — to another teenager to use. I had reconciled myself to not being able to ride on this move. I could still look at the landscape, I could roll down the window and smell the sweet air and feel the breeze and the sun on my face, and occasionally I could stop, get out, and stroll around a bit in the grass.

We always made it a practice to stop for a meal when we reached that stretch of pure unbroken prairie. The riders would dismount and hobble their horses or tie them to the fence, I'd park the truck, Peter would throw down a couple of hay bales for a table or for people to sit on, and I'd put out the lunch. We'd sit in the sun and eat sandwiches, and his mother's baked beans, the pot wrapped in layers of newspapers to keep it warm, and drink coffee from thermoses. Long before we reached there I'd have begun to look forward to that moment.

I discovered what the annual day spent crossing these acres of prairie meant to me when, as we were about to begin that part of the trip, a circumstance arose — I don't even remember what it was — that meant somebody had to drive one of the men the twenty or so miles around the fields, down the roads and wait with him there at the corrals for the riders and cattle to arrive. Since Peter could hardly order anybody else to do it, and nobody volunteered, it was taken for granted that as his wife I would leave the drive and take this man where he needed to go.

I wanted to protest, but I couldn't bring myself to do it in front of so many people, especially since arguing or complaining are just not done on a trip like that. It would be a little like a sailor telling the captain of a ship that he didn't feel like taking the watch that night. My true feelings were too private to speak out loud, and I couldn't come up with any practical reason why I shouldn't have to that didn't hint of adolescent pique or, not knowing how the others felt about the prairie — but the fact that nobody volunteered to go should have given me a hint — that I could be sure anybody but Peter would understand. And everyone else was a volunteer; I was official staff. I knew I wouldn't be able to go back and catch up with the drive, either. For me, for that year, the drive was over.

I got back in the truck and started driving, trying to smile, trying to make conversation, while all the time I was fighting back tears. I wanted so badly to spend that last few hours on the prairie, the only time we ever went through those fields, that I had an actual pain in my chest as I drove away and that stayed with me till I went to bed that night.

I said about that incident much later to a friend, "If everything happens to teach you something, why was that taken away from me? What was I supposed to learn from that?" and answered my self, "To teach me how much the wild prairie means to me." Years later, I was able to go further: to understand how precious it is, how unique, how deeply it might affect one, changing even one's understanding of life.

Sometimes I think I'm still not over that loss. Especially since, during the good times, farmers bought all that land the rest of the gang travelled over on horseback that day, and plowed it up to turn it into a farm. Now, ten years later, the farming operation is failing, but you can't turn plowed-up shortgrass prairie back into the original terrain. It's gone forever, or given a human life span, as good as forever, along with the wildlife that lived on it.

It occurs to me now to wonder if perhaps the very real — and surprising even to me — sorrow I felt that day as I drove away, and all the rest of the day and for days afterward, wasn't perhaps intuitive, if perhaps a part of me knew that I would never again experience the sweetness of that air, the sun warm on my face and hands, the view so vast the soul felt free, because by the next spring or the spring after that it would be gone forever.

As the years passed, I felt more and more that the best comfort I had was in being in the landscape. I was only mildly curious about how the prairie was formed, and when and how it was evolving, and I certainly had none of the interests of ecologists or environmentalists. I was merely looking at the prairie as a human being, savouring it for its beauty which engaged all the senses and brought with it a feeling of well-being, contentment and often even joy.

My approach was to simply wander in it with no particular destination, to lie in the sun and bury my nose in the sweet-smelling grasses and forbs such as sage, to admire the colours and textures of the sedges, shrubs and succulents which make up the mixed grass prairie, or to sit on a slope looking out across miles of prairie to the horizon, watching the shifting of shadows and light across it, thinking no thoughts that, a moment later, I would remember. I was there only to enjoy the prairie. I asked for nothing more, not thinking there was anything more.

I had only the most cursory interest in the names of the plants, although Peter's mother taught me a few of those which flowered: scarlet mallow, three-flowered avens, gumbo primrose, golden bean, which she called "buffalo bean," and which someone else told me she knew as the wild sweet pea. I could hardly miss the wild rose or the prairie sunflower, and I knew a few others such as the wild licorice and the wild morning glory and anemones which grow along the riverbank, from my childhood in the north. Peter showed me the greasewood, badger bush and club moss and pointed out the two species of cactus — the prickly pear and the pincushion — and much later I learned from a rancher's wife (herself a rancher and also a poet) that if you had the patience to gather the berries, you could make cactus-berry jelly. I taught myself a few: the many types of cinquefoil and sage, and milkweed, and the Canada thistle with its purple flower that a saddle horse — "Watch this," Peter said — would clip tidily off with its bared teeth, never touching a barb. I longed to see a field of wild prairie lilies as I had in my childhood in the north, but I never have, not even a single flower growing wild in the grass.

Because we had a hay farm, I learned to identify a number of grasses — timothy, bromegrass, foxtail — and legumes — clover, alfalfa — which I saw every day, some of which were imported species, crested wheat grass, Russian wild rye, and many of which, like reed canary grass, were very beautiful. I attended three-day-long range schools with Peter, one in the Bears Paw Mountains of Montana, but I did so chiefly for the adventure and to spend an entire day on the prairie instead of only a few hours. At these schools I learned to identify death camas when I saw it, and a few of the many native species of grass — needle-and-thread grass, June grass, blue grama or buffalo grass — and a forb or two.

Other seasons brought different pleasures. All one snowy winter I walked a mile down the riverbed every morning with the dog trotting ahead, flushing out cattle from the banks or far back around the last curve where the fenceline crossed and stopped them, then chasing them up to the feed-grounds where Peter and his hired man were throwing out hay, grain bales and grain itself. For two winters the snow was so deep that it muffled sound so that the cattle which had sought shelter in these snug places couldn't hear the tractor and didn't come out for feed. Or sometimes, looking back, I think Peter came and got me each morning to make that walk out of understanding that I needed to feel useful, a part of the operation, and that if I spent all of each day inside that tiny log house I would soon be "bushed," develop cabin fever, be impossible to live with — that I might leave.

I remember those walks each morning as among the best of my life. I would head down the riverbed, following in the tracks of the cattle where the snow was too deep to walk comfortably in. The banks of the river are high and steep, and the winds had pushed the snow into deep banks that overhung the edges of the cliffsides in fat lips of snow that looked like waves on the ocean and from which long icicles sometimes hung. Looking up from the snowy riverbed, I saw white walls of snow and then the snowy billows and beyond them the brilliant sky. I saw the places where partridges snuggled up for the night to keep warm and followed the tracks of coyotes and foxes and animals whose tracks I didn't recognize. I was picking up knowledge, hardly even noticing that was what I was doing. Running to cut off a cow, I fell headlong in the snow and, with no one watching me, lay there laughing, blinking up at the sky, losing myself in its blue depths.

For most people the worse the weather is, the more likely they are to stay indoors; not so for old-fashioned ranchers — for them the worse the weather, the more likely the rancher is to be out in it, in the midst of blizzards searching for cattle out on the prairie and chasing them down into the shelter of deep coulees, or home to the windbreaks and corrals. On such days I went along with Peter and learned again that the human limits of endurance are much greater than day-to-day life has us believe; that is, I became less afraid of the weather at the same time as I became a good deal more respectful of it.

One of the first Christmas gifts Peter gave me was a pair of cross-country skis, and as long as there was enough snow, which there usually isn't in this desert country, I'd be out on the prairie in the winter, too, skiing. I began to take my skis and go out into the hills during storms, having discovered that I liked storms for the way they changed the appearance of familiar places and for the sense of mystery they brought to them.

Memories of my childhood came back to me: playing in the bush with my friends, with my sisters and cousins in our grandmother's garden, skating on frozen sloughs in winter till the pain from the cold became so bad even we kids couldn't stand it anymore and went home, the winter we had built a snow fort that lasted for months as we added on and made it more and more substantial so that it stood well into spring. I felt like a child again, had fleeting moments when I remembered how wonderful the world itself had once seemed, and how it was to be cared for, worry-free, and living in the body again and not just the mind.

And I was recreating myself as a writer. I not only was meditative by nature, this having been developed in me as the result of being an extremely shy and retiring child in a big family, I had also developed in me the seeds of the observer. It was a lucky thing, although I'd never have admitted it then, to have arrived a stranger in a strange land, when I was no longer young, with a touch of the observer's cold eye already in my makeup.

I found myself observing the very people with whom I seemed to have so little in common. I saw the people of my new community as different from those of the rest of the province, and I was surprised to discover that they themselves seemed to define themselves as different, although nobody ever explicitly said so, in that they often had closer links both in terms of lifestyle and in family ties to Alberta and to Montana than they did to Saskatchewan. Many of the families had begun as Americans and had close relatives on the farms and ranches over the border and in Alberta, and when young people went off to higher education or trades schools or to jobs, when I first came here, they were much more likely to go to Alberta than to Saskatoon or even Regina. As a group they seemed to me often to think more like western Americans or like Albertans, with that essentially conservative, independent cast of mind, than they did like the good-old-Tommy-Douglas-prairie-socialist school of thought to which I belonged and which had always seemed to me to define Saskatchewan.

I soon discovered, in my attempt to tell the story of these people and this place, that my fund of facts, of precise knowledge, was inadequate to the task I'd set myself. Each story, each book, each play would become an exercise in information gathering. When Peter couldn't answer my questions I turned to books. Peter took me to meet old people, old men who'd pioneered in the area, and I listened to their stories and made notes, and where it was possible, which was practically never, I tried to match their memories to the scant written history I could find.

I carried a notebook everywhere. Chasing cows home on bitter winter days, I'd stop the truck, get out, draw a little diagram of the way an animal had pushed away the snow from a sage bush, write a description of the bush and the snow and the droppings the animal had left, the colours, the place where the sun was in the sky on that day at that time and how the cattle looked. I wrote the last few pages of *The Gates of the Sun* sitting on a straw bale in the back of the pickup in a neighbour's field while I waited for Peter to finish baling the straw, pausing in my scribbling only to ask questions of Peter and the neighbour, when they stopped for coffee, about what was a native species, whether bird, animal or plant, and what wasn't. It constantly amazed me how much the men knew.

With every story and every book I was forced to search out new information. My fund of information, of facts, obtained in all these ways — my own observations, Peter's answers to my incessant questions, the stories of old people, books — was growing. Without intending to or even really wanting to, I was becoming knowledgeable about the history of the area and its plant and animal life. Although I will never know all there is to know — Peter still knows a thousand times more than I do — having begun by being transported by its beauty, and then being overwhelmed by my sense of loneliness and purposelessness, I was at last starting to feel at home in the terrain, at home in the landscape. Of course, I didn't see this as it was happening, but by learning to name things in my new environment, by discovering the scheme of the place and the way the parts fit together, I was making them my own, and by this I was slowly healing myself.

Years later when I was the expert instead of the neophyte, a friend and I were out walking in the rain. In this semiarid country where rain is rare and precious, walking in it is exhilarating, imbued even with a touch of magic. We came to a place where a pair of great horned owls sat watching us, and as my friend went closer to see them better, I sat in the grass in my leaky boots and a borrowed yellow rain jacket which came to my knees, not minding the wet, looking out over the misty fields, noticing how everything smelled different because of the moisture, how colours had changed and intensified.

I thought of how my friend and I had moved over the wet ground, where we had gone and not gone, what we had found ourselves doing, and suddenly I realized that it was the land — Nature — that had guided our steps, made our choices for us, and not the other way around. That is, because we were friends and rambling in the countryside for the pleasure of each other's company and for the pleasure of being out-of-doors, having no set plan or goal, we had gone where the shape of the land had suggested itself to us; we had done what the land had made available to us. If it was too muddy or wet in one place, we went somewhere else; if a hill was too steep, we went around; there was no way to cross the river without swimming and it was too cold to swim, so we followed its course instead and sat on its bank.

I thought, then said, "This land makes Crees of us all." By this, I meant that it appeared to me that the Crees, for example, developed the culture they developed because it was the best fit between themselves and the land. And it was the land that taught them that. They adapted to the land, and not the other way around as we Europeans so stupidly did, trying to force this arid western land to be, as government propaganda had for seventy-five years and more put it, the "breadbasket of the world."

I began to think about the ways in which land affects the individual, or at least this particular landscape, the Great Plains of North America. I began to see that in our human arrogance we assume we can affect the land but it can't affect us — except in practical ways: hurricanes, floods, drought — when there are plenty of ways we might find that the land — Nature — is affecting us without our being aware of it. In considering the differences between Peter and myself, I had not imagined or considered the possibility that he had been shaped by the land, by Nature, that in subtle ways we've never identified nor even really talked about, his psyche itself had been shaped by Nature not merely by his observation of it but by its subtle, never described or even consciously realized, influence on him.

The Great Plains landscape is an elemental one. There is little natural water in the form of lakes or rivers or even ponds, no forests, no mountains — just miles and miles of land and a sky across which weather visibly, majestically passes. One winter visitor to this place said it reminded him of the high Arctic where he had once lived, and several others, Wallace Stegner included, spoke of the plains of Africa. The landscape is so huge that our imaginations can't contain it or outstrip it, and the climate is concomitantly arbitrary and severe.

It is geology stripped bare, leaving behind only a vast sky and land stretched out in long, sweeping lines that blend into the distant horizon with a line that is sometimes so clear and sharp it is surreal, and sometimes exists at the edge of metaphysics, oscillating in heat waves or, summer or winter, blending into mirages and the realm of dreams and visions which wavers just the other side of the horizon. The Great Plains are a land for visionaries, they induce visions, they are themselves visions, the line between fact and dream is so blurred. What other landscape around the world produces the mystic psyche so powerfully? Sky and land, that is all, and grass, and what Nature leaves bare the human psyche fills.

It was not until I moved into the country to live that my significant dreaming really began. I did not think about this fact, but if I had, I am sure I would have explained it as a by-product of the radical change in my way of life. Eventually it was suggested to me by an eminent western Canadian writer in whom I had confided that perhaps living in this ancient, skeletal landscape had brought on these dreams. At the time I reserved judgement, but a few years later, in another context, another western Canadian writer told me how she had, after years of living in the city where she didn't believe she had dreamt at all, moved out into the country and suddenly began having vivid, meaningful dreams. She attributed these to the influence of the landscape in which she now made her home.

In the context of these remarks it seems to me very significant that dreams have always held an important place in Aboriginal cultures of the Great Plains of North America, as they have in many other such cultures around the world. Aboriginal people take the content of their dreams as simply another source of information about the world, a guide for action,

48

and as prophecy, either in their individual lives or as directives to their communities. In these cultures it is considered extremely foolish, a great insult, even a sin, to ignore an important dream.

Prophetic dreams are accepted at face value and are used as a basis for action. A South Dakota writer living near Rapid City told me that a few years ago Chief Crazy Horse — whose name I'm told should more accurately be translated as "Enchanted Horse," or "Vision Horse" — appeared in dreams to the elders of his nation to warn them about an imminent flood on a branch of the Cheyenne River. The flood did occur and it killed more than a hundred of his people who lived along its banks. Hugh Brody, in *Maps and Dreams*, describes a hunting culture, the Beaver Indians of northeastern British Columbia, where the best hunters are guided by dreams to their kill; the very best hunter-dreamers have even dreamt the way to heaven and then, awaking, have drawn the map.

Although I sometimes go for long stretches without any dreams that seem important to me, a few years ago I began to have the occasional prophetic dream myself. I dreamt the San Francisco earthquake a couple of weeks before it happened. Since I'd never been to San Francisco, I thought the city in the dream was Vancouver and the broken bridge, the Lions' Gate. Although it was a powerful enough dream to tell people about it, I certainly never took it as prophecy until I saw the broken span of the bridge on television. It was identical to the one in my dream where it had been the main icon. I dreamt of the Japanese airplane that lost its rudder and, after weaving drunkenly through the air for half an hour, crashed into a mountain. I was in bed dreaming it as it was happening. When I got up the first thing Peter did was to tell me about this terrible event that had just happened in Japan. I even dreamt of the death of one of the Russian Communist leaders a few days before he died. It may be that I've had more prophetic dreams than I know but simply haven't remembered. Actually I think this may be true of everyone, but most people don't record their dreams as I usually do, and so forget them.

I have described the dream I had in which a giant eagle and a giant owl appeared to me. It became for me a life-dream, a significant dream that launched me on a journey through comparative religion, mythology, the study of dreams, psychoanalysis, and finally into the study of the nature of the female. At an archetypal level, it is a dream about masculine power, symbolized by the soaring eagle, and feminine power, symbolized by the owl standing near me on the ground. In beauty and power they are exactly equal, but I, a woman, had spent my life to this point following the eagle — that is, accepting masculine interpretations of life in general and, of my own life, accepting masculine goals and taking masculine desires for my own — instead of cleaving to the owl, searching out and coming to terms with my own feminine soul.

My search for understanding of the dream led me into and through my novel *Luna* — the story of the lives of contemporary ranch and farm women and how they live, feel about, and understand their rural, agricultural, traditional lives — and from there into my short story collection *Fever*, a much more personal and urbanized study of the same issues. It's been a good dozen years since I had that dream and I still run across further ways to interpret it. Not only have I accepted it as guidance in the direction my life has taken, it is, to a degree, the foundation on which I have built the rest of my life.

I think that significant dreaming is one way in which Nature influences and changes the individual, developing in her/him an awareness of Nature as more than mere locale, or a setting, a context, as more than beauty, as more than something that is merely Other.

It was in Joseph Campbell's *Primitive Mythology* that I first heard of Aboriginal dreamtime, and not long after, in a much more firsthand and compelling way in *The Lost World of the Kalahari* by Laurens van der Post. All peoples of the earth have creation stories of one kind or another. The stories of prescientific peoples tell variously of a time when the world was in the process of being created along with the creatures on it. This was a timeless time, a time before time, when animals, plants and people could become one another and the formations of the earth were taking shape. It is called, in mythologies around the world, dreamtime, and out of it springs stories and legends about archetypal creatures, sometimes gods, whose manifestations remain now in the fallen time.

It seems, too, that on some level this timeless time still exists in another realm, and those people peculiarly blessed — including, but never exclusively, shamans — may still go there. In this realm many strange things can happen: animals can converse with humans and vice versa; the dead may appear and speak, or creatures from the dreamtime thought by some of us to be merely metaphoric. The earth becomes more beautiful, approaches, even achieves, perfection, and everything in it and on it is imbued with meaning. And especially the sense of the ticking of time vanishes.

I believe that since Aboriginal people around the world have nontechnological cultures and live in and by Nature — or at least, once did when their cultures were developing — and these cultures had developed the concept of dreamtime and took dreaming very seriously whether in New Zealand, Australia, the Kalahari Desert of Africa, or the Great Plains of North America, that surely it was Nature which, whether with will and intention or not, taught, allowed, gave them dreams as an instrument of knowledge.

I began to see from my own experience living in it that the land and the wild creatures who live in it and on it, and the turning of the earth, the rising and setting of the sun and the moon, and the constant passing of weather across its surface — that is, Nature — influenced rural people to make them what they are, more than even they knew.

Close proximity to a natural environment — being in Nature — alters all of us in ways which remain pretty much unexplored, even undescribed in our culture. I am suggesting that these ways in which such a closeness affects us, from dreams to more subtle and less describable phenomena, are real, and that we should stop thinking, with our inflated human egos, that all the influence is the other way around. We might try to shift our thinking in this direction so that we stop blithely improving the natural world around us, and begin to learn, as Aboriginal people have, what Nature in her subtle but powerful manner has to teach us about how to live.

More and more I am coming to believe that our alienation from the natural world is at root of much that has gone so wrong in the modern world, and that if Nature has anything to teach us at all, her first lesson is in humility.

Explorations

Anna Brownell Jameson
(1794 – 1860)

Anna Brownell Jameson spent nine months in Canada (1836–37) during an attempted reconciliation with her husband, Robert, who was the Attorney-General of Upper Canada. She was already a well-known writer and advocate for women's rights in England. Although the marriage did not survive, Jameson turned the experience of her Canadian sojourn into a memoir of explorations in **Winter Studies and Summer Rambles in Canada.** *In addition to bringing the exotic backwoods of Canada to an English audience, Jameson recorded feats such as shooting rapids never before attempted by a European woman. After this experience, described as more heady than two glasses of champagne, Jameson was given a new name by her Native hosts. The renaming suggests the transformation that occurred to her in and through the wilderness experience. On her return from the summer rambles, she quickly came to a separation settlement with her husband and returned to England, where she continued her literary career and campaigned for expanded educational and employment opportunities for women.*

It was very beautiful

from *Winter Studies and Summer Rambles in Canada* (1838)

The more I looked upon those glancing, dancing rapids, the more resolute I grew to venture myself in the midst of them. George Johnston went to seek a fit canoe and a dextrous steersman, and meantime I strolled away to pay a visit to Wayish,ky's family, and made a sketch of their lodge, while pretty Zah,gah,see,gah,qua held the umbrella to shade me.

The canoe being ready, I went up to the top of the portage, and we launched into the river. It was a small fishing canoe about ten feet long, quite new, and light and elegant and buoyant as a bird on the waters. I reclined on a mat at the bottom, Indian fashion (there are no seats in a genuine Indian canoe); in a minute we were within the verge of the rapids, and down we went with a whirl and a splash! — the white surge leaping around me — over me. The Indian with astonishing dexterity kept the head of the canoe to the breakers, and somehow or other we danced through them. I could see, as I looked over the edge of the canoe, that the passage between the rocks was sometimes not more than two feet in width, and we had to turn sharp angles — a touch of which would have sent us to destruction — all this I could see through the transparent eddying waters, but I can truly say, I had not even a momentary sensation of fear, but rather of giddy, breathless, delicious excitement. I could even admire the beautiful attitude of a fisher, past whom we swept as we came to the bottom. The whole affair, from the moment in [sic] entered the canoe till I reached the landing place, occupied seven minutes, and the distance is about three quarters of a mile.

My Indians were enchanted, and when I reached home, my good friends were not less delighted at my exploit: they told me I was the first European female who had ever performed it, and assuredly I shall not be the last. I recommend it as an exercise before breakfast. Two glasses of champagne could not have made me more tipsy and more self-complacent! As for my Neengai, she laughed, clapped her hands, and embraced me several times. I was declared duly initiated, and adopted into the family by the name of Wah,sah,ge,wah,no,qua. They had already called me among themselves, in reference to my complexion and my travelling propensities. O,daw,yaun,gee, the fair changing moon, or rather, the fair moon which changes her place; but now, in compliment to my successful achievement, Mrs. Johnston bestowed this new appellation, which I much prefer. It signifies the bright foam, or more properly, with the feminine adjunct qua, the woman of the bright foam; and by this name I am henceforth to be known among the Chippewas.

> The total descent of the Fall of St. Mary's has been ascertained to be
> twenty-two and a half perpendicular feet. It has been found
> impracticable to ascend the rapid; but canoes have ventured down,
> though the experiment is extremely nervous and hazardous, and
> avoided by a portage, two miles long, which connects the navigable
> parts of the strait.
>
> – Bouchette's Canada

July 31

This last evening of my sojourn at the Sault Ste. Marie is very melancholy — we have been all very sad. Mr. and Mrs. MacMurray are to accompany me in my voyage down the lake to the Manitoolin Islands, having some business to transact with the governor: — so you see Providence does take care of me! How I could have got there alone, I cannot tell, but I must have tried. At first we had arranged to go in a bark canoe; the very canoe which belonged to Captain Back, and which is now lying in Mr. MacMurray's court-yard; but our party will be large, and we shall be encumbered with much baggage and provisions — not having yet learned to live on the portable maize and fat: our voyage is likely to take three days and a half, even if the weather continues favourable, and if it do not, why we shall be obliged to put into some creek or harbour, and pitch our tent, gipsy fashion, for a day or two. There is not a settlement nor a habitation on our route, nothing but lake and forest. The distance is about one hundred and seventy miles, rather more than less; Mr. MacMurray therefore advises a bateau, in which, if we do not get on so quickly, we shall have more space and comfort — and thus it is to be.

I am sorry to leave these kind, excellent people, but most I regret Mrs. Schoolcraft.

August 1

The morning of our departure rose bright and beautiful, and the loading and arranging of our little boat was a scene of great animation. I thought I had said all my adieus the night before, but at early dawn my good Neengai came paddling across the river with various kind offerings for her daughter Wa,sah,ge,wo,no,qua, which she thought might be pleasant or useful, and more last affectionate words from Mrs. Schoolcraft. We then exchanged a long farewell embrace, and she turned away with tears, got into her little canoe, which could scarcely contain two persons, and handling her paddle with singular grace and dexterity, shot over the blue water, without venturing once to look back! I leaned over the side of our boat, and strained my eyes to catch a last glimpse of the white spray of the rapids, and her little canoe skimming over the expanse between, like a black dot; and this was the last I saw of my dear good Chippewa mamma!

Meantime we were proceeding rapidly down the beautiful river, and through its winding channels. Our party consisted of Mr. and Mrs. MacMurray and their lovely boy, myself, and the two Indian girls — my cousin Zah,gah,see,ga,qua, and Angelique, the child's attendant.

These two girls were, for Indians, singularly beautiful; they would have been beautiful anywhere. Angelique, though of unmixed Indian blood, has a face of the most perfect oval, a clear brown complexion, the long, half-shaded eye, which the French call *coupe en amande*; the nose slightly aquiline, with the proud nostril open and well defined; dazzling teeth — in short, her features had been faultless, but that her mouth is a little too large — but then, to amend that, her lips are like coral: and a more perfect figure I never beheld. Zah,gah,see,ga,qua is on a less scale, and her features more decidedly Italian.

We had a small but compact and well-built boat, the seats of which we covered with mats, blankets, buffalo skins, cloaks, shawls, &c.: we had four voyageurs, Masta, Content, Le Blanc, and Pierrot; a very different set from those who brought me from Mackinaw: they were all Canadian voyageurs of the true breed, that is, half-breed, showing the Indian blood as strongly as the French. Pierrot, worthy his name, was a most comical fellow; Masta, a great talker, amused me exceedingly; Content was our steersman and captain; and Le Blanc, who was the best singer, generally led the song, to which the others responded in chorus.

They had a fixed daily allowance of fat pork, Indian meal, and to-bacco: finding that the latter was not agreeable to me, though I took care not to complain, they always contrived, with genuine politeness, to smoke out of my way, and to leeward.

After passing Sugar Island, we took the channel to the left, and en-tered the narrow part of the lake between St. Joseph's Island and the main land. We dined upon a small picturesque islet, consisting of ledges of rock, covered with shrubs and abounding with whortle-berries; on the upper platform we arranged an awning or shade, by throwing a sail over some bushes, and made a luxuriant dinner, succeeded by a basin of good tea; meantime, on the rocky ledge below, Pierrot was making a galette, and Masta frying pork.

Dinner being over, we proceeded, coasting along the north shore of St. Joseph's Island. There is, in the interior, an English settlement, and a village of Indians. The principal proprietor, Major R —, who is a magis-trate and justice of the peace, has two Indian women living with him — two sisters, and a family by each! — such are the examples sometimes set to the Indians on our frontiers.

In the evening we came to an island consisting of a flat ledge of rock, on which were the remains of a former camp-fire, surrounded by tall trees and bushes: here we pitched our little marquee, and boiled our kettle. The sun-set was most glorious, with some floating ominous clouds. The stars and the fireflies came out together: the latter swarmed around us, darting in and out among the trees, and gliding and sparkling over the surface of the water. Unfortunately the mosquitoes swarmed too, notwithstanding the antipathy which is said to exist between the mosquito and the firefly. We made our beds by spreading mats and blankets under us; and then, closing the curtain of the tent, Mr. MacMurray began a very effective slaugh-ter and expulsion of the mosquitoes. We laid ourselves down, Mrs. MacMurray in the middle, with her child in her bosom; Mr. MacMurray on one side, myself on the other, and the two Indian girls at our feet: the voyageurs, rolled in their blankets, lay upon the naked rock round the fire we had built — and thus we all slept. I must needs confess that I found my rocky bed rather uneasy, and my bones ached as I turned from side to side, but this was only a beginning. The night was close and sultry, and just before dawn I was wakened by a tremendous clap of thunder; down came the storm in its fury, the lake swelling and roaring, the lightning gambolling over the rocks and waves, the rain falling in a torrent; but we were well sheltered, for the men had had the precaution, before they slept, to throw a large oil cloth over the top of our little marquee. The storm ceased suddenly; daylight came, and soon afterwards we again embarked. We had made forty-five miles.

The next morning was beautiful: the sun shone brightly, though the lake was yet heaving and swelling from the recent storm — altogether it was like the laughing eyes and pouting lips of a half-appeased beauty. About nine o'clock we ran down into a lovely bay, and landed to breakfast on a little lawn surrounded by high trees and a thick wood, abounding in rattlesnakes and squirrels. Luckily for us, the storm had dispersed the mosquitoes.

Keeping clear of the covert to avoid these fearful snakes, I strayed down by the edge of the lake, and found a tiny creek, which answered all purposes, both of bath and mirror, and there I arranged my toilette in peace and security. Returning to our breakfast-fire, I stood some moments to admire the group around it — it was a perfect picture: there lay the little boat rocking on the shining waves, and near it Content was washing plates and dishes; Pierrot and Masta were cooking; the two Indian girls were spreading the tablecloth on the turf. Mrs. MacMurray and her baby — looking like the Madonna and child in the "Repose in Egypt" — were seated under a tree, while Mr. MacMurray, having suspended his shaving-glass against the trunk of a pine, was shaving himself with infinite gravity and sangfroid. Never, I think, were the graceful, the wild, the comic, so strangely combined! — add the rich background of mingled foliage, the murmur of leaves and waters, and all the glory of a summer morning! — it was very beautiful!

Mary T. S. Schaffer
(1861 – 1939)

Mary Schaffer was another explorer of Canada who came in search of the wildflowers of the Rockies. Born in Pennsylvania, she received artistic training including tutelage under the American flower painter George Lambden. As well, she was an accomplished photographer. Accompanying her husband Charles, who was doing a botanical study of the plants of the Rockies, she recorded the specimens in paintings and photographs. After his death, she returned to the Rockies, having convinced Stewardson Brown, Curator of Herbarium Academy of Natural Sciences in Philadelphia, to help complete the project. The resulting Alpine Flora of the Canadian Rocky Mountains *was published in 1907. Like Anna Jameson, Schaffer encountered many adventures not meant "for a lady." Despite the trials of roughing it, Schaffer made several trips to the Canadian West and is credited with being the first non-Native person to discover Maligne Lake in the Rockies.*

A Maiden Voyage on the "New" Lake

from *A Hunter of Peace* (1911)

The camp-site just mentioned was a lucky find. How the men ever fell over it I cannot imagine; but they had a Robinson Crusoe sort of habit of falling over the right thing at the right time, and at the moment we scarce wondered. It must have been half a mile back from the river; we rode through fierce scrub to reach it, but once there the horses were as safe as though corralled. The feed was knee-deep and inexhaustible, and we shook ourselves into quarters with the idea of several days' stay.

With the lake now found, fresh food for conversation developed. A high double-peaked mountain, with a very large glacier on its north face, could be seen above the tree-tops about thirty-miles distant. It seemed a little too much to the north-east to be Mount Brazeau, while the one that "K." reached in his climb seemed too far to the south-west. Both were in splendid view and kept us guessing.

The Botanist quickly grew busy; he had struck a botanical haven, very rare specimens of other sections of the mountains were there in masses, and other plants he had not seen at all were there also. Dinner passed off with the exciting intelligence that "tomorrow will be devoted to building a raft, as the shores, as far as can be seen, are impassable for horses, and it must be fully three miles to the head of the lake. We will then take tents, blankets and food for three days, and you enthusiastic climbers can fight it out from the top as to which is Mount Brazeau."

Our part of the raft-making next morning was the uncommon permission to wash up the breakfast dishes, and the three men were soon swallowed up in the trees as they went down to the lake, each with his axe over his shoulder. With things snugged up and a huge pot of pork and beans set to simmer over the fire, I too strolled down. It was a stroll, too, that took about a half hour to do the job, as the fallen timber made it hard travelling and the sloughs near the lake were boot-high. But we didn't make rafts every day or even reach a spandy-new lake, so the exertions seemed well worth the cause. As I came quietly out to the water's edge, there were two of the men out in the lake busily lashing two logs together, and "K." was just rounding a point gracefully riding a dead tree, which, at that moment, as gracefully rolled over and landed him in the water. He was, however, already so wet that he couldn't be much wetter, so he shook himself amidst a momentary smile all round, and shoved his old tree into place.

I found a dry spot and sat watching them come and go for an hour. "Chief," who was an accomplished axeman, wielded his axe with an artistic ability interesting to see; and as I looked at them all, working almost in silence, my mind went back to the first carpenters who had cut logs in those waters — the busy little beavers whose work was still visible, but whose pelts had been the cause of their extermination.

At six o'clock the three men walked into camp, soaked, of course, but jubilant over results, and announced that *H.M.S. Chaba* would sail for the upper end of the lake tomorrow morning at nine.

A short pow-wow after supper resulted in learning that we were to go in style regardless of our plea that we were willing to rough it for a few days; air-beds, tents, and food for three were to be taken on that raft.

Personally my sensations towards large bodies of water are similar to those of a cat, and though I begged to rough it, it was not so much to do something uncomfortable as to keep from drowning on an overtaxed raft. With qualms and misgivings next morning, I watched bags, boxes, and bundles carried out and deposited on the upper deck of the *Chaba*, the last two packages being "M." and myself, who were dumped unceremoniously on with the rest of the cargo. The Botanist waded out for himself, as did Muggins, the rowers climbed aboard, and we set sail. Now that she was loaded, the lower deck looked alarmingly under water, and "M." and I were seated high on a bag of flour, a slab of bacon, and bundles of blankets. To the novice in rafting, nothing could have looked more insecure or unreliable; wide gaps in the logs showed unmeasured depths of green water below, and it seemed as though, with a sudden lurch or sharp turn, we must be shot from our perch into the cold, unfathomed waters.

Determined to put up a brave fight, I clutched my log and awaited a spill. It never came; she rode as steady as a little ship and as slow as a snail. She was propelled by two sweeps twelve feet long; the men took twenty-minute turns at her, the rest of us looking on and silently wondering at the fearful task and lack of complaint. At noon she was paddled as near shore as possible and all hands landed for lunch; Muggins, who sat at the tip end of the landing-log, voted the performance a terrible bore, and nearly jumped out of his skin when once he reached terra firma.

Back once more on the raft after an hour's rest, the men slowly pulled the clumsy little craft, foot by foot, past exquisite bays and inlets, the mountains closed more and more about us, and at six-thirty, as we seemed within a mile of our goal — the head of the lake — we hove to, and camped by a stream which came from the double-peaked mountain. Landing, we found our new home was a garden of crimson vetches. As the warm winds swept across them, the odour brought a little homesick thought of the sweet clover-fields of the east in July.

Opposite our camp rose a fine snow-capped mountain down whose side swept a splendid glacier. As we paddled slowly in sight of it, "K." suddenly looked up and said, "That is the mountain from which I first saw the lake." So we promptly named it "Mount Unwin." Though the breath of the vetches remained with us all night, the thought of home fled with the crash of avalanches from Mount Unwin's side, and the distant yapping of coyotes in the valley behind us. With the coming of the morning, our plans were quickly laid to paddle the intervening mile to the end of the lake, take a light lunch, then climb for the keynote of the situation — Lake Brazeau.

On one point we had found Sampson's map very much at fault: he had both drawn and mentioned "narrows" about two thirds of the way up the lake. These had never materialized and we commented on the fact of finding Sampson seriously at fault. The raft was growing to be so homey and reliable a vehicle that even the timid now stepped gaily aboard, all but Muggins; he hated that raft, and came aboard sighing and dejected as though he had been whipped, but of course had no intention of being left behind, and away we sailed with a pack-mantle hoisted to catch any passing breeze.

In about an hour, as we were rounding what we supposed to be our debarking point, there burst upon us that which, all in our little company agreed, was the finest view any of us had ever beheld in the Rockies. This was a tremendous assertion, for, of that band of six of us, we all knew many valleys in that country, and each counted his miles of travel through them by thousands. Yet there it lay, for the time being all ours — those miles and miles of lake, the unnamed peaks rising above us, one following the other, each more beautiful than the last. We had reached, not the end of the lake, but the narrows of which Sampson had told us. On our left stood a curiously shaped mountain toward which we had worked our way for two days. We called it "The Thumb"; next rose a magnificent double-headed pile of rock, whose perpendicular cliffs reached almost to the shore. Its height? I've no idea. It was its massiveness, its simple dignity, which appealed to us so strongly, and we named it "Mount Warren," in honour of Chief, through whose grit and determination we were able to behold this splendour.

As we slowly advanced beneath the shadow of "The Thumb," a large fissure, at least 1,000 feet above us, became visible, and from it there burst a fine waterfall. So great was its drop that it became spray, waving back and forth in the wind, long before it touched the rocks below, then gathering itself in a little stream, tumbled headlong into the lake, losing itself in a continuous series of ringlets.

After four hours of tough rowing, we reached the head of the lake, and landed for lunch on an old alluvial fan. None of the higher peaks were here visible, the supposed Mount Brazeau south of us, the uncertain Mount Maligne east of us, or even Mount Unwin; they were all hidden by lower shoulders of themselves.

Like feudal lords (and ladies) we sat at our mid-day meal of tinned-meat and bannock that day. Our table, the clean sweet earth itself, was garnished with flowers, with vetches crimson, yellow, and pink. They spread away in every direction from us as far as the eye could see, and, the warm winds blowing down upon us from the southern valleys, swept across their faces and bore their clover-laden breath to the first white guests of that wonderful region.

With lunch over, we wandered about to drink it all in. How pure and undefiled it was! We searched for some sign that others had been there — not a tepee-pole, not a charred stick, not even tracks of game; just masses of flowers, the lap-lap of the waters on the shore, the occasional reverberating roar of an avalanche, and our own voices, stilled by a nameless Presence.

We wanted a week in that heaven of the hills, yet back at "Camp Unwin" was only one more day's grub, so, scolding at Fate, we turned toward *H.M.S. Chaba* as she lay indifferently swashing her cumbersome form against an old beached log, whose momentary duty it was to prevent her from drifting off across the lake.

As we came up, Chief had just chopped out a smooth surface on the side of a small tree, and there, for the first time and only in all our wanderings, so far as I can remember, we inscribed our initials and the date of our visit.

Even then I think we all apologized to ourselves, for, next to a mussy camp-ground, there is nothing much more unsightly to the true camper than to see the trees around a favourite camping site disfigured with personal names and personal remarks, which never fail to remind one of the old adage taught the small boy in his early youth when he receives his first knife.

And one more name we left behind, not carved upon a tree but in our memories. All day the thought of one who loved the hills as we did ourselves was in my mind, and though she could not be with us, yet did I long to share our treasures with her. On the lake's west shore rose a fine symmetrical peak, and as we stepped cautiously aboard our craft (I never could get over the idea that she would go over with a sneeze), I said: "With every one's sanction I call that peak Mount Mary Vaux." There was no dissenting voice.

Foot by foot we left it all behind — the flowers, the tumbling avalanches, the great rock masses we had named, the untraversed valleys, and the beautiful falls.

The day was dying fast; as we glided by the tempting coves, and swept through the narrows — now "Sampson's Narrows," — the setting sun touched a symmetrical snow-tipped peak on the eastern shore of the lake, the dark waters before us caught up the picture, threw back to us an inverted rosy summit, and we named it "Sampson's Peak" for him who had sketched us the little map. The heavy rhythmic breathing of the rowers and Muggins's occasional sighs were the only drawbacks to absolute and perfect enjoyment; but for the tense faces before us and the tenser muscles, we could have looked ahead and aloft and said,—"This is Paradise."

As we came into port under the shadow of Mount Unwin, the sweet odour of the vetches came out to greet us, the sun sank behind the hills, the winds died away, every ripple of the lake disappeared, even the mosquitoes ceased to bother us; The Thumb, Mounts Warren, Unwin, Sampson, and many other unnamed peaks were dyed in crimson, which changed to purple, to violet, then night with its cloak of darkness fell. As the evening's camp-fire was lighted, there came across the water the distant bark of a coyote, overhead passed a few belated duck; except for these there seemed no other life than that of our little family hidden there in the wilderness where "home" had never been before.

The weather on Sunday morning, July 12th, refused to take any action on all adverse signs of the previous evening and burst upon us clear, bright, and best of all, calm. There is little joy in the prospect of a trip on a large mountain lake with only a few logs between you and the depths below, and a storm either imminent or in progress, so every one was thankful. The day was warm, it became absolutely hot; by 8:30 camp equipment and all hands were each in their allotted space, the steady splash-splash of the sweeps broke the glass-like surface about us, and the mountains and islands reflected in the lake, cast about us a fairy-land as we pushed away from them into broader waters. After tying up for a short rest and lunch, we arrived at our original starting-place at 6 PM, thus ending probably the first voyage ever taken on Maligne Lake.

On reaching land we turned and took a last look at our little craft. Built without nail or spike, held together with wooden pegs and lash-ropes, every ugly line in little *H.M.S. Chaba* was endeared to us. She had carried us far and safely, and now, with regret, we left her there on those lonely shores where other travellers some day may find and use her. Returning to our original camp we found all well and in order, and in an hour no one would have realised we had just returned from a maiden voyage.

The next day the homely duties of washing and mending engaged some of us, while others searched for a trail to the lower end of the lake. The night of the 13th was one of the worst we had ever endured in camp. Heat and a brewing storm brought out every mosquito for miles around I am sure. Donning our hats and "bug-nets," we stowed ourselves away in the suffocating sleeping-bags, expecting the usual change before midnight. Nothing came but more mosquitoes, which hummed and howled and prodded the protecting net till sleep became well-nigh impossible. Toward daylight I rose in my wrath and, with a swoop, switched out a perfect cloud of the brutes, hit "M." on the nose, and woke her unintentionally from a sound sleep — the sleep a marvellous fact to me considering the circumstances.

We then and there vowed to get even with our tormentors, so the minute breakfast was over, out came the netting, nail-scissors, and shoe-thread. While I measured and sewed, "M." hovered over me with a big balsam bough which she kept switching, and by afternoon we could sit placidly in our tents and defy the thousands of impudent little bills presented at our front door.

Home

Laura Beatrice Berton
(1878 – 1967)

Laura Beatrice Berton travelled to the Yukon to take up a job as a school teacher. What was to be a short term stay turned into a much longer commitment with her marriage to Frank Berton. The couple was separated during the first World War and after Frank's return had to face the challenge of the stagnating economy of the North. Torn between their love for the land and the difficulty of surviving, they decided to try to remain. Berton describes the beauty and difficulty of life in the North particularly for women. In this section she records the birth of her famous son Pierre.

Chapter 10

from *I Married the Klondike* (1954)

When the war ended and Frank returned safely we had a major decision to make about our lives. Would we settle Outside, renouncing the Yukon for ever, or would we go back to the dying Klondike? It was a hard decision to make, but in the end the North won. I know that the phrase "the spell of the Yukon" has become a cliché since Robert Service first coined it, but that does not make it any the less powerful. Certainly, we spent long hours discussing plans for settling down in the fruit lands of Ontario or among the roses of Vancouver Island. But we both knew, deep down inside ourselves, that the Yukon was our life and we could not give it up.

There is a phrase in the North which people still use about those who cannot bring themselves to leave. "He's missed too many boats," they will say. Well, I guess Frank and I had missed too many boats. I had only meant to stay in the Yukon one year; he had gone, long before me, to stay just two years. Now we were preparing to go back again for the remainder of our lives.

I think as we talked over our plans that the thoughts of both of us harked back to a certain summer's day almost a decade before, in the early days of our marriage. It comes back to me now as sharply as if it had all happened yesterday. We had struggled for hours up a steep, tangled gulch, our feet deep in wet caribou moss and our legs and ankles bruised by sharp rocks. Then, suddenly, we broke out on to a sunlit hillside. On its upper reaches, fairly dancing with the joy of life, was a grove of young white birches. Lower down, towards the valley, lay acres and acres of wild flowers — clumps of blue lupines, larkspur five feet tall, monkshood and great feathery bunches of white Baby's Breath. We never spoke of that scene to each other again, but it was one of the reasons why we were returning.

But we did not go back immediately to Dawson. Instead, Frank found himself transferred to Whitehorse as Government agent. Here he held the posts of mining recorder, fire warden, inspector of weights and measures, and half a dozen other jobs all rolled into one. We arrived, typically enough, on an October day late in 1919 in the midst of a blinding blizzard.

Whitehorse was still the sleepy little town I had first seen twelve years before on my way into the Yukon. Its population still stood at three hundred — three hundred that is before the boat crews and ships' carpenters and those townspeople lucky enough to take a winter holiday had left for the Outside. When the snow came Whitehorse was like a deserted village.

It was a neat, tidy community, in sharp contrast to Dawson, built on volcanic ash and clay. There were few tumbledown or boarded-up shacks, no piles of mining machinery, no weed-choked ditches. It was bordered by the headwaters of the Yukon on one side and a low plateau on the other. We ate plenty of mountain sheep in season, and it was possible to get salad greens all winter each time the coast boat docked in Skagway. The eggs were fresher, and therefore, to Dawsonites, insipid. After the rich orange storage eggs, these tasted quite flat. There was also more sunshine in the winter, for we were three hundred miles farther south. Even on the shortest day we could still see our shadows.

Whitehorse was also a quieter town than Dawson. It was, indeed, a typical northern small town with no metropolitan aspirations. Dawson was in no sense typical of anything — it was unique. Whitehorse was pretty well a company town, for the White Pass and Yukon Transportation Company kept it going. The social climate was not the same as in Dawson and there was bitter rivalry between the citizens of the two towns, as is often the case in neighbouring communities. (In the Yukon three hundred odd miles is still "neighbouring.") White horse felt it was neglected by the Federal Government and claimed Dawson "hogged everything." To Dawsonites, Whitehorse was nothing more than a jumping-off place and they made no secret of their superiority. I must say I got the impression that Dawson people were none too welcome in Whitehorse and certainly in the time we were there we kept pretty much to the Dawson crowd.

Politics was partly responsible for this. Whitehorse was a Liberal town; Dawson was now Conservative. The Blacks, indeed, used to claim that they had to sneak through Whitehorse from steamboat to train, hiding their faces as they went. This was melodramatic overstatement, for as a matter of fact the Blacks were often tendered a reception and a dinner in

Whitehorse. All the same this was the general impression. Political distinctions were so carefully drawn that our friends warned us when we arrived to divide our patronage carefully, when buying provisions, between Capt. Paddy Martin's grocery and general store (Liberal) and Taylor and Drury's emporium (Conservative). Throughout our two years in Whitehorse we systematically dealt with one shop one month and then, in the next month, with the other.

In this atmosphere we were glad to see anybody from Dawson, or, indeed, anyone who was at all familiar. We soon struck up an acquaintance with, of all people, Dolly Orchard, the ex-dance-hall girl, and her husband, Jimmy Turner, who had been the subject of considerable gossip in Dawson. The last we had heard of them she had been taking in miners' washing on the creeks to make ends meet, but now he had a good Government job. Dolly had become a Christian Science healer and was well liked by the townspeople. She still had the same wonderful hair and alluring eyes that had made her the toast of the dance-halls, but no mention was ever made of her gaudy past. It turned out that among other people she had cured my first Yukon escort, Mr. Hamilton, of alcoholism. I had last seen him standing drunkenly on the river bank as our boat pulled away from the shore. Now he was a frequent and sober visitor to the town.

The only connecting link between Whitehorse and the Outside was the little narrow-gauge railway running over the White Pass to Skagway. The train came in twice a week during the winter unless, as seemed perennially the case, it was snowbound, blocked by a rockslide or a flooded river. When this happened our isolation was complete. There was no fresh milk, for all the cows were in Skagway. There was no mail and usually no telegraph service, for in periods of bad weather the wires were down. There was no undertaker, for he too came from Skagway.

One winter while we were in Whitehorse a trapper was frozen to death outside his cabin several miles downriver. A patrol of police went out to bring in the body. Unfortunately the wretched man had met his death while struggling to open his cabin door. His arms were outstretched and his legs spread-eagled. The undertaker happened to be in town when news of the tragedy came out, so in order to save an extra trip he remained in Whitehorse to prepare the corpse for burial. But when the frozen cadaver was brought in by sleigh he faced a problem: how to bury a spread-eagled corpse in a Christian coffin. The only answer was to wait while the body slowly thawed, a process that took longer than anybody imagined. The impatient undertaker had to miss several trains.

Train day was an event in Whitehorse. It meant mail, fresh milk, green vegetables, strangers in town. And during the summer when one of the semi-weekly steamboats was also in town waiting to take its load to Dawson to connect with the Lower River steamers en route to Fairbanks, Alaska, the town really woke up. It was considered no more than a patriotic duty for every true Whitehorse booster to swell the crowd at station or dockside. As one socialite explained to me shortly after my arrival, "I think it's our duty to show the tourists that we're not all Indians and Eskimos and that we know how to dress decently."

In the winter of course it was the Overland Stage that connected with the train. Its facilities had been greatly depleted since I had made my journey to Dawson a decade before. There were fewer travellers to the mining camps now, for the palmy days were over. Many of the road-houses which in the old days had been spotted every twenty-two miles along the winter road were closed. Passengers now had to provide their own lunches and these were eaten in the open after being thawed out by a bonfire on the side of the trail. In the old days we had made the journey in less than a week. Now the stage only made a post a day and, if the trail was bad, the trip often took longer than a fortnight.

This was too long for many men and there were great numbers who preferred to walk to Dawson with their goods on their backs, following the tracks of the stage in the snow. We had not been long in Whitehorse before Arthur Coldrick, the Englishman who had been on the stage when I travelled aboard it, arrived in town from the Outside.

"I'm walking in, you know," he said, talking as casually as if he were about to take a stroll down Regent Street. And off he went, in his brisk way, on a three-hundred-and-sixty-mile hike through deep snow, lonely forest, frozen river and high plateau, in the dead of winter with the thermometer well below zero and the blue Aurora his only beacon. A short time later we had a letter from him from Dawson, describing the experience. He spoke glowingly of the climate and the scenery, but less enthusiastically of the sleeping-quarters, which had certainly degenerated. He told us about one place where all the stage passengers slept in a large stable divided by a canvas-partitioned room in the centre. He said he didn't mind mice rummaging around his feet, but the strong smell of ammonia from the horses made sleep difficult.

We had not been in Whitehorse three months before I realized that after eight years of marriage I was going to become a mother. After my years of handling other people's children I was to have one of my own. But my satisfaction was leavened by some slight feelings of anxiety. Whitehorse had a much smaller and more primitive hospital, devoid of the facilities of the larger institution in Dawson. The doctors had a habit of flitting in and out of town like bees moving from flower to flower. And I was no longer young. I was forty-two years old, facing my first baby. Nor was I heartened by the fact that the two Dawson kindergarten teachers who had followed me on the staff and had later been married had each died in child-birth at a younger age. I could see my friends looking at me queerly and a little tragically, as if I were already marked for death, and could almost hear them whispering, behind my back, "Will she make the third in a row?"

But my greatest worry, during the months of waiting, was the town doctor. He just wouldn't stay put. I started out with one doctor but he left town within a month or two under tragic circumstances. His wife had died of influenza and the events attendant on her death were particularly grisly. While the poor woman was still alive it had been necessary to summon the undertaker from Skagway to stand by until the end came. Otherwise he would have missed his train again. As a result of this, the doctor had no stomach for Whitehorse and he departed.

Now we were without a doctor and the town's health was entrusted to the care of the druggist's assistant, as the druggist himself was Outside for the winter. I was decidedly dubious about going to him for obstetrical care, for it seemed to me that he had more experience selling picture postcards of Robert Service's cabin than he had in the practice of pharmacology.

It was two months before Doctor No. 2 arrived. He was a fine-looking man and the town liked him. Unfortunately we liked him better than he liked us, for at the end of the month he took himself off and once again we were at the mercy of the drug-store clerk.

My time was drawing near when Doctor No. 3 arrived, heralded by numerous reports as to his ability and experience, not to mention the inevitable details about his background, family, spare-time pursuits and lovelife, which were all tied up neatly in the verbal parcel of information which preceded every new arrival into the North.

I received my summons on a hot July day when the flies were thick and the dogs lay sleeping in the dust of the main street and the thermometer stood at ninety-two in the shade. I walked briskly to the hospital, showing a boldness I did not feel, accompanied by husband, dog and a thick horde of mosquitoes. The hospital was almost as empty as the grave; the only other occupant was an elderly Indian being treated for a carbuncle.

Now began a curious ordeal. The windows of my room opened on to the main street and as my pains began to increase in regularity and sharpness I became aware of a conversation being carried on by two women standing on the sidewalk below. They were old acquaintances, one an ex-schoolteacher married to a White Pass official, and the other the wife of the principal, a stout, florid Englishwoman of fifty named Mrs. Fortesque, who had a passion for grotesque Victorian hats and a great love for tittle-tattle. She especially loved to go calling, for she clung tenaciously to the social forms which had been drummed into her as a girl in an English cathedral town. She called on all newcomers within two weeks of their arrival in town, and when anyone left town she called again. She called on brides with good wishes, on the sick for speedy recovery, on mourners with deepest sympathy. Immaculately gloved and bearing her antique card-case, with the proper inscription for the proper occasion written in a flowing script in the upper left-hand corner, Mrs. Fortesque was always on hand with congratulations or condolences when fortune smiled or disaster befell. As the pains engulfed me I became aware of the fact that without a doubt Mrs. Fortesque and her friend were discussing my approaching death, and I began to wonder whether they had already sent for the undertaker from Skagway.

Now the whole question of women in the North crossed my mind again, as it had during my lonely hours on Sourdough Gulch. I could not help but think of poor Mabel McIlwaine, who had succeeded me as kindergarten teacher and had died in child-birth. And Mabel Magwood who had followed her. She married John Henry, the shy science master whom I had first met on my trip into the Yukon. He had planned a dream honeymoon in the wilds of Swede Creek, up the Yukon, where they would live in a tent and commune with nature. Alas, it had all been too much for Mabel, and half-way through this idyllic period she had dragged him back to town again, thoroughly fed up with the nomad's life that so many men and so few women in the Yukon enjoyed. She did not trust the land. When she became pregnant, she determined to have her child Outside. She went to a proper hospital and there, ironically, she too died of childbirth.

The whole situation made me furiously angry. I decided that come what may I would spite the chattering women on the street corner and live through my labour. My expression became ferocious and I think it quite startled the nurse who now entered. The baby was coming and she was sweating as profusely as I when suddenly a knock came on the door. The nurse swore, rushed to the door and shouted: "Go away! Go away!" In the hallway I could just spy, out of the corner of my eye, that familiar Victorian hat. The nurse returned, looking grim and bearing an engraved calling card on which Mrs. Fortesque had written, in her beautiful script, the words "With kindest enquiries." I am sure she had a second one ready for Frank "With deepest condolences."

A few moments later the doctor arrived and delivered me of a healthy baby boy. But before I was out of hospital, he too had fled the town. I really think the poor man was distressed by the excellent health of the towns-people and departed for sicklier climes. He was replaced sometime later by Doctor No. 4.

We brought the baby up in the kitchen of our bungalow. My mind reverts to it today whenever I see the sleek, modern kitchens which have nothing at all visible but drawers, cupboards and handles. My own kitchen in the north was a sort of G.H.Q., the most important room in the house. It was here that the whole family, dog included, took its weekly Saturday night bath. It was here that the Monday wash was soaked and wrung out and dried on a complicated arrangement of ropes and pulleys suspended from the ceiling. It was here that the man of the house shaved and here, in the fall, where he brought home the kill from the hunt and butchered it for winter's use. The kitchen was dining room and den and now, on top of everything else, it became a nursery.

The child's first year was normal enough, enlivened only by occasional hazards peculiar to the Yukon. It was my habit to set him out in the yard on the crisp spring days when there was still plenty of snow on the ground, tying him securely in his pram and giving him a bread crust to gnaw on while I worked in the kitchen. But one day when I did this I was disturbed by a loud cry from him and on going out found the crust gone. I gave him another but in a few moments it had vanished, too, and he was crying again. The crusts continued to disappear as fast as I gave them to him and it was only when I watched from the window that the mystery was solved. Quick as a wink a great Canada jay swooped down, seized the bread from the child's hands and made off with it while he looked on with an expression half of fear, half of interest on his face. In the Yukon the bird is colloquially known as Camp Robber and rightly so. He is the boldest bird I know.

The baby's closest friend, our dog Grey Cloud, looked more like a wolf. This was not surprising, for his grandfather had been a timber wolf. He had a soft, long-haired coat — silver grey with highlights of amber — and a magnificent tail that curved over his back like a graceful willow plume. He had a gentle but tragic expression and there was nothing of the wolf about his temperament. He was a pacifist among dogs, a canine philosopher who enjoyed quiet walks in quiet places and hated the fierce, sudden fights that sprang up like passing squalls in the streets of the town. There always seemed to be one of these dog fights going on, involving several huskies all tearing at each other in a tight ball of fur and teeth. When Grey Cloud sighted one of these brawls he would pretend not to see it, but holding his head high would look intently in front of him until we were well past. He liked nothing better than to accompany the baby and me as I wheeled him through the quiet woods behind our cabin.

These walks in midsummer were often marred by the presence of mosquitoes and black flies, which were far worse in Whitehorse than in Dawson. It is almost impossible to describe to those who have not experienced it the fearful ordeal of walking through these swarms of insects that, in the early days, quite literally drove unprepared men insane. During the height of the fly season we simply could not venture outside the house without wearing a thick head-dress of black chiffon which covered our heads and came down tight around our shoulders. Without this, existence out of doors was pure and simple hell. In addition it was important to wear gloves and heavy stockings so that every possible square inch of bare flesh was covered. Before our days at Whitehorse came to an end we believed the story of the mosquitoes which attacked a man carrying home a copper wash-boiler. Unable to cope with them, he took refuge inside the boiler, only to find that they were stinging him right through it. Desperately he seized a rock and hammered each stinger as it came through the metal. At this the insects rose up in a cloud and, finding themselves securely fastened down, flew away taking the boiler with them.

Before we left Whitehorse and were recalled to Dawson, the first aeroplane flew into the North and landed on a plateau above the town. The entire village flocked up the hill to look at the strange machine, which seemed to be all wire and struts. Nobody could know then that the aeroplane would be the making of Whitehorse, that this wild, wooded plateau would one day become the biggest airfield in the North, that the sky over the town would become black with planes and that while Dawson slowly shrank on the banks of the Klondike, Whitehorse would rise to a wartime population of thirty thousand men, building the Alaska Highway and Canal pipe-line system and manning the North-West Staging Route to Alaska. Whitehorse's day was yet to come, but that day was still a long way off. When we left it, the town was still a thin line of frame buildings acting as a stepping-stone between the Outside world and the Klondike.

Theodora Stanwell-Fletcher
(1906 –)

Theodora Stanwell-Fletcher earned degrees in literature and animal ecology with a PhD from Cornell University. In addition to her many scientific and natural history articles, she wrote accounts of her exploration and settlement in wilderness areas. Driftwood Valley *is the journal of the creation of a wilderness home on Tetana Lake in the remote Driftwood Valley of British Columbia between 1937-41. She and her husband John were employed by the British Columbia Provincial Museum to collect and identify the flora and fauna of the area. They looked on the opportunity as a professional challenge but more importantly as an opportunity to realize their dream of living as closely as possible on and from the land. Their experience and the way in which it fundamentally altered their outlook and values is recorded in* Driftwood Valley *which won the John Burroughs Medal for nature writing in 1947.*

A Northern Spring

from *Driftwood Valley: The Northern Frontier* (1946)

Tetana

April 4

The snow is sinking fast and bare ground shows around many of the trees. But in the woods it is still six feet deep. We may have to wear snowshoes for another month. The Indians say that one has to wear them even in June in woods across the river. Tetana is the only lake anywhere around even partly free of ice. The open water patches should prove an attraction to migrating birds.

After a winter almost completely windless, except for a few short light breezes, high winds from the southwest are now sweeping up across the valley. They hurl themselves down the lake in mighty gusts and threaten to toss our cabin on the way. We're greatly alarmed about our roof, which has now some odd patches of flimsy roofing paper added to it. More than once we've climbed up on the roofing to hold it down by main force. Thus far we've been successful.

The jays and chickadees are coming less frequently to the feeding station. Necessity for food is less; they are absorbed in love-making and mating and nest building. An injured red squirrel has been around. One front paw hangs useless, and such a forlorn, thin little bunch of misery it is. One day it was creeping humbly about picking up crumbs, when a big healthy squirrel pounced on it and started tearing it to pieces. J., in a fury, promptly shot the attacker. The poor little hurt one, all bleeding and bitten around the mouth, hobbled away.

I suppose, by all the laws of Nature, we should have destroyed the weak and preserved the strong, so much better able to cope with life. Is man's instinct of chivalry toward the weak, unfit ones really a sign of progress and wisdom, or isn't it?

Old Bear Lake Charlie came yesterday. One of his little girls cut off the end of her finger with an axe. Her hand has apparently become infected and she is very sick. She "talk, talk, all the time and see bad things." He wanted us to ask Michelle, if he returned this way from his trap line, to hurry with the dogs to the Bunshaw cabin so that they could take the child to Bear Lake. He said to tell Michelle that he thinks "mebbe he [she] die" because "he dream about big chief long time dead and see him come." Charlie said he has "cut many people" and always put on beaver castors, which make the wounds heal. Now he has no beaver castors and is "very sorry."

Michelle and Mac arrived today. When we conveyed their father's message, they gulped and, tears in their eyes, hurried off without stopping to visit. These Indians seem devoted to their families and full of consternation and pity when any accidents or illnesses occur. We often wonder if they would have any real sympathy for us if we fell into bad circumstances. I believe that perhaps they would, just at first. Once at Bear Lake, when J. was stunned from a fall on ice and we thought that he might have been badly hurt, I was surprised to see tears and a spasm of pity on Selina's face. But pity, I imagine, would be short-lived. They would probably say, "By gosh, too bad that man [or that woman] he hurt [or he die], but I can't do nothing!"

J. claims that all natives are fatalists, far more so than the white man. When, in times past, he has been caught in dangerous ventures with the Eskimos, he says that after a time the Eskimo, convinced that he will die, lies down on the job and no longer bothers himself, The white man, on the other hand, will go on fighting long, long after there is no apparent hope, or until he is no longer capable of physical action.

We invite nearly every Indian who arrives at our cabin to come in for hot tea and bannock. Some white people of this country, with their strong feeling of racial superiority, believe this to be a bad precedent. Theoretically and ideally I think they are wrong. Practically, situated as most of them are, perhaps they are right. However, we do not live in a community, or run a trading establishment. We are alone, and acquire our livelihood from the wilderness as these Indians do. We are their neighbours and would behave as such. J., accustomed to the Far North where everyone is always given a hot drink, insisted that we do likewise here. At first it seemed to me rather unnecessary. Since I always boil cups and spoons to guard against t.b. or venereal disease, it makes considerable trouble. But now that I understand travelling in this country, I realize just what warm drink and nourishment mean at the end of a hard trip. J. and I would, moreover, like to return in some small measure the hospitality of the Indians. Wherever we have gone in this country these people have been invariably generous about offering to share their homes and food with us. In this respect, at least, they are more hospitable to the white man than the white man is to them.

April 8

The northward migration of birds has begun at last. Two days ago we went snowshoeing at 5 AM when the crust was still hard enough to hold us. The mountains had flushed dawn-pink at 4:30 and sunshine was coming out through spruces across Tetana. The temperature was 20. Life and warmth and spring were abroad. Down the lake in the still air, three wolves gave voice with soft lazy whines. One, with a yawn and a stretch and a good-natured howl to clear his lungs, was perhaps just waking. Another, which we now call "the boy soprano," gave suddenly the lovely, clear, high note which always drops down to the soft sad one. A male pine grosbeak, his body deep rose, was singing a rippling carol in the willow by our cabin.

Late in the afternoon of the day which had begun so still and clear and beautiful, the wind changed. In no time at all it rose to a gale, and driving, needle-sharp rain descended. At twilight, at 7 PM, there was a loud, sudden flapping against the cabin wall outside, like a tent shaking in a gale. It was two American mergansers, a dark female and a georgeous [sic] black-and-white male. With great difficulty they got down under wind and landed in the open patch of water below the bank. They must have been about to head down to the lake when a gust flung them against our cabin.

Yesterday, despite heavy wet snow all morning, followed by rain in the afternoon, a killdeer, calling plaintively, arrived at the edge of the water. At dusk, in hard rain, three mountain bluebirds came to the bank. There was just time, before darkness fell, to see the heavenly blue of their backs and their light breasts.

Today a robin was singing, and after the robin there came from the pine grove clear, metallic little sounds, like someone striking tinkly notes on a harpsichord. We crept out with glasses and found a varied thrush. Except for the rough dark band on its red-brown breast, it is something like a robin. There has been a pair of Brewer's blackbirds, also new to us, but easy to identify. The male has a purplish head, white eyes, and green metallic body, and the female is gray-brown. Tiny kinglets, yellow and orange crowns stuck up like jewels, are hopping on the shed roof and big spruce tree. A large shore bird, with streaked breast and long sharp wings, paused for one second on the willow bush and was off before we could get a real look at it.

The weather is so cold and dull it must be discouraging to the new birds. But longing for love and mating and the summer nesting ground is more compelling than all the difficulties of long flight through any dangers.

The little hurt squirrel which J. saved is still around. Now it looks as though it might survive and be fairly healthy after all!

April 10

For a week the weather has been atrocious. Rain every day; pile upon pile of dirty melting snow, and unlovely debris are being uncovered all about us. We're completely confined to the cabin and to the few yards around it where we've dug snow away to keep from being flooded out. Getting wood and water and shovelling are our only exercise, but they furnish plenty. We can't go anywhere, even on snowshoes, without sinking through slush above our knees. Paths leading to wood and water have been packed so hard that they now stick far up above the rest of the melting snow. They look safe to walk on, but twice, when I've gone along them without snowshoes, which don't really seem to be much help, my feet have gone through. I've sunk to the waist and had a fight to get out.

One day when J. was in bed with lumbago, the first real illness either of us has had, and I was going for wood, one leg sank way down and my foot was caught tight. I tried to dig it out with my hands. The more I pulled and twisted, the more packed snow-ice formed around it. If I had had my big knife! But it was in the cabin. Who could think of desperately needing a knife in the fifteen yards between the house and the woodpile? Poor J., unable to straighten his back, crawled moaning out of bed and, though scarcely able to move, hacked my foot and leg out of its plaster cast with an axe.

Despite bad weather the spring bird migration goes on steadily. No need for us, in typical ornithologist fashion, to travel forth, build a "bird blind" to match the scenery, and squat for hours inside it in an agony of cramped limbs, watching birds from tiny peepholes. Our cabin, which most of the birds apparently now accept as part of the landscape, serves as a perfect blind and we can watch the water just below in comfort from our windows.

Tetana, with its open patches at the north and south ends, is still the only open water anywhere around, and is proving a favourite way station for the birds. The birds drift steadily now up the Driftwood Valley, new species by ones or twos, or even small companies. Many, having come hundreds or thousands of miles north, travelling successfully without calendar or compass by day or night through all kinds of weather, will arrive at their summer homes on approximately the same date as they have done for years. When the birds leave Takla, still icebound, thirty miles away, the first water, other than tiny patches on the river, is Tetana. Here there is space for water birds; even a small shore line, free of snow, for land birds. In the dark stretch of forest and snow-covered wilderness, bounded on two sides by an endless sea of mountains, Tetana must lie like a haven of rest.

Yesterday morning when we woke, we saw from our pillows a Townsend's solitaire sitting on the clothesline by the open window. Though we have never before seen one alive, we knew it from the pictures. The large, soft gray bird, with slight yellow markings on the flight feathers, the thrushlike head and bill were unmistakable. One of our great ambitions is to hear the "heavenly music" of the solitaire, which nests in high mountain solitudes. Perhaps when we climb the mountains this summer it will be there.

Four male pintail ducks, their beautiful, cleanly shaped little brown heads striped with white, and tail feathers lengthened into long sharp points, have arrived; and for five consecutive nights around six-thirty, the same mergansers have come to our pool. We can set our clock by them. Tonight they were joined by another pair, and what a flutter they all fell into! The two males chased one female and then the other. And once the ardent lovers had a serious fight. They grappled each other with long narrow bills, and sank completely under water, the salmon pink of their undersides (which appears chiefly in courtship plumage) conspicuously gorgeous. Then the females turned the tables and chased them, spurning first one male and then the other. Such a squawking and opening of mouths and sticking up of defiant tails, one never saw. But they have finally settled it peacefully, for now, in the darkening twilight, they are sleeping calmly, four heads tucked under four wings, a male and a female side by side.

April 11

Last night was warm and still, with a gentle fine misty rain. The partly full moon shone with a watery light. Just as we were going to sleep, around eleven, we were surrounded suddenly by the music of trumpets, deep and sweet and melodious. We almost fell from our beds, and when we hung out the window, there in the shining silver mist were four great, white, graceful swans, long necks and huge wings lit by the moon. They were slowly circling our cabin and the pool. Now they were out above the water, now low close over our roof. In bare feet we padded from window to window, hushing little Rex, who was rumbling in his throat at this new sound. The swans almost decided to land. Perhaps the area of open water is too small, perhaps the cabin frightened them, for, after some little time, they floated like small white angels up into the northern sky, rising ever higher and farther till they had disappeared. Then came more trumpeting high up, and we saw the tail end of a "V" formation of a dozen swans flying northwest. Long after they had all melted into the white misty night we could hear the fairylike horns and trumpets receding into the distance.

We feel sure that these could have been no other than the rare, almost extinct trumpeters. For never was there a more perfect reproduction of professional trumpeting. The notes were so strikingly low and soft, so clear and resonant, yet exquisitely modulated.

Yesterday afternoon a lonesome female Barrow's golden-eye was with the two pairs of mergansers, who ignored her utterly. This morning, a male Barrow's golden-eye has joined her. There could scarcely be anything more splendid. We can hardly stop gazing at the royal purple of his velvet head set with topaz eyes and half-moons of white, the beautiful patterned black and white of his body and wings.

April 17

After the last few warm days, snow has begun to slide on the mountains. There is a sudden soft swish followed by a thunderous roar, like an express train hurtling by. Then an echoing, softer roar down the valley, succeeded by a shocking quiet. The old giant of the mountains is giving voice at last, and well that Tetana lies a good six miles away. No wonder the Indians give these mountains a wide berth in the months of melting snow. One of the great fears of their lives, in addition to grizzlies, rutting bull moose, and breaking through thin ice, is the possibility of being buried by a snow slide.

Often at night we're waked from sound sleep by the noise of an avalanche. In the dark the roar sounds greater and deeper and more terrifying.

Last night at 2 AM, I saw a miracle! Great, bright scarlet clouds were rolling over the pinewoods. My first sleepy thought was of fire. Then I realized that such a thing couldn't be, for there is still a blanket of wet snow, feet deep, for hundreds of miles around. It must be a new manifestation of the aurora; but instead of the usual streamers and zigzag curtains, great rolls of cumulous clouds seemed to bear the lights. The crests were flame-red; the white Driftwood and the white snow everywhere were painted crimson. Clear sky over the mountains was a pale, glowing green and yellow. The colours were too intense to be dimmed by even a brilliant full moon. Where snow has melted across the lake leaving bare ice, it was glittering gold, and the open water was half gold, half green and red. Black silhouettes of wild ducks (ordinarily so noisy and lively now throughout all the night hours) were passing slowly in complete silence in long lines up and down the water, leaving wakes of gold and scarlet ripples.

I could never have even imagined such a sight! It was all unbelievable, the sort of thing that happens only in fairy stories. But I know it was real, because I walked all round the house and moved a chair or two. J. was in one of his dead sleeps and refused to wake. But since he says Northern Lights are no better than sunsets, I wasn't sure that he deserved to wake anyhow.

Small companies of crows, which we haven't seen since last fall, have come back again. And sometimes there is the deep guttural quauk-quauk of a big raven, as it flies ponderously above the cabin. One day when we were crossing the meadow we saw an evening grosbeak on a tall spruce. The black and yellow velvet of its markings, the heavy pale blue bill, were unmistakable. We were wildly excited at this remarkable visitor, so far north of its range; and J. tried, without success, to collect it. At his first shot a whole company of shrill, yapping coyotes, who must have been following us closely, began to howl defiance.

Yesterday morning we took a walk down the lake at five, our snowshoes clattering on the hard lumpy crusts. Dozens of ducks were in the open water at the outlet. The mallards, heads gleaming emerald and violet in the morning sun, had their funny little black tail feathers standing coquettishly up in stiff, lacquered curls. Incidentally the Indians tell us that mallards are the only species of duck in this region which are sometimes caught in traps set for beaver and muskrat. There was a dainty green-winged teal, with a green and cinnamon head and white and gray body; and both the American and the Barrow's goldeneyes with green, or purple, plush heads and white and black velvet bodies. Pintails and baldpates arrived while we were there. The baldpates have white foreheads like bald old men, and pink and gray sides. When we got back to the cabin, a flock of violet-green swallows, newly arrived, gleamed like iridescent peacock-coloured jewels, as they darted up and down over the water.

This morning was clear and still and we were off again at six over toward Trail Lake; then north to the meadow. Suddenly way down the valley there was music, for all the world like a travelling calliope, coming gradually nearer and louder. On the southern sky appeared a gigantic "V" of trumpeters — seventy or more — the dazzling sun lighting their white bodies as they passed low just above us, headed slowly for the northwest. Through the low, resonant trumpets and soft bugles came soft, short little notes, made, we supposed, by the young cygnets. A golden eagle swooped down and up in great wide arcs, but the lovely, eager swans paid him no attention as they sang their way along.

The antics and distinctive habits of the different kinds of ducks make royal entertainment. The most noisy and conspicuous are mergansers and goldeneyes. The additional Barrow's goldeneyes — there are now four pairs — have added complications. The males, in an ecstasy of showing off, stand straight up in the lake, weaving their purple heads from side to side and shaking their wings. When they fly through the air, or volplane thirty yards across water, their wings make a shrill whistling noise which distinguishes them from other ducks, even after dark when we can't see them. The little brown-headed lady goldeneyes remain quiet and demure, outwardly unperturbed by the antics of their passionate swains. They are not bold and aggressive and modern, like the lady mergansers.

The tiny green-winged teal surprise us by giving voice to a plaintive sweet whistling note, completely unlike the noises one commonly associates with a duck. The teal are busily employed gobbling up early insects — springtails and a tiny gnat — which are over snowbanks and above the water.

Pintails and baldpates, especially the latter, appear to have considerably less skill in flying and landing than other ducks. The baldpates land so clumsily and awkwardly that we can tell them half a mile away.

For the first time we have seen fresh skunk tracks, and smelled a strong skunk smell, on the north side of the meadow. We have been told that an average of twelve skunks are brought in annually at Bear Lake, and the Indians say that in every case the skunk is caught in a marten trap set. Whether this is owing to the bait or scent used, or the type of brush shelter under the trees where the trap is set, it is hard to say.

April 24

The lake is almost completely open at last. I had forgotten how lovely are reflections of blue sky, white mountains, and green forests. And we have a boat. It is one of Charlie's dugout canoes, hauled down on the snow from Bear Lake by Charlie's dogs. We bought it for $25 and are immensely pleased with it. It's thirty feet long and is made, as are all dugouts in this country, from the trunk of a huge balsam poplar. After a careful selection of the tree the Indians fell it, and then start a slow fire inside. When the fire has partially hollowed out the trunk, the rest of the shaping and cleaning process is continued by axe and knife until there is a smooth, shapely interior. Wooden stretchers are wedged across the two ends and middle, and it is ready for use. If the boat is badly balanced, big stones are placed in its bottom. We find our dugout is no more difficult to steer and balance than an ordinary canoe. The chief difference is that it is much heavier and harder to lift.

We are able now to explore the lake to our hearts' content, and I suppose that my adventuresome husband will soon be off on the dangerous river. Two pairs of little bufflehead ducks arrived last week. The males, with fluffy, pure white pompoms on their heads, bear themselves as proudly as kings. Several large companies comprising seventy and eighty swans have gone over. We are sure these were the whistlers because of their distinctly higher, more whistling-like notes. Though some notes were lovely and musical, they completely lacked the deep resonant character so marked in the trumpeters. Grouse are beginning to drum back in the woods (we have suddenly begun to see ruffed grouse now as well as Franklin's). And there are marsh hawks, sharp-shinned hawks, a kingfisher, and a Lincoln's sparrow.

The tiny, striped, gray-headed chipmunks have waked from their seven months' sleep; they all appeared around the twentieth and are scampering about, tails erect as usual, as sleek and fat as if they had been feeding steadily for half a year. Now their favourite food is pussy willows. They climb up in willows along the bank and make a pretty picture as they sit nibbling at a pussy head.

May 5

We're all excited because Basil Holland, a Takla Indian with a trap line southeast of the Kastberg, brought a surprise packet of mail from Takla. Mother and Dad may take a trip west this summer and if they do will come away off up here to pay us a visit. Just at present we can talk of nothing but the joy of showing them this country. But if they come west, will they really surmount all the hazards of travel in this land and be able to reach us? We sent out, to be mailed by Basil next week at Takla, voluminous epistles of advice, and directions, and urging; all of which had to be written in the course of a few hours between lengthy conversations and eating and drinking, because Basil had to start back in the early morning.

This is so typical of this country. Weeks and months go by without our even remembering that such a thing as mail exists. Except for a visit about once a month from the odd Indian, who knows no more of the outside world than we do, and whose quiet coming and going scarcely disturbs the even tenor of our ways, we almost forget that there is an outside world. Then suddenly, completely unexpected and unannounced, someone arrives with a several months' (often they are four to six months old) batch of letters and business matters. And they all have to be decided upon and answered in a few hours, unless one wishes them to slide for another four to six months. The person who brings them is full of talk and news which we want to hear. So, only the most important business communications are answered, and those in such a confused and haphazard form that people whose aim in life is Business, carefully and accurately performed, wonder if we have taken leave of our senses and gone completely wild! The personal letters don't get answered at all (they've waited around for months anyhow) because most of our friends and relatives will have given us up entirely.

Open ground everywhere now, except in thick woods; and oh! the joy of being able to walk without snowshoes again and feel the ground under our feet. Little Rex, longing for spring greens, gobbles up every blade of new grass — and then gets sick.

The Driftwood, nearly freed of ice at last, is rising. J., strutting like a turkey gobbler, appeared with a six pound Dolly Varden, caught in the river near Tetana's outlet after a thrilling battle with snags and currents. The fish are beginning to run. The tender, pale pink flesh of the trout tastes heavenly. We're heartily sick of stale strong moose meat.

Willow buds and poplars are showing bright new green, the mountains above the thick timber still shine with deep fresh snowfalls, but the lower slopes are green, laced with a thousand new white foaming streams. The limpid green and blue and purple of the waters of Tetana are a rest to eyes unspeakably weary from gazing on unsullied whiteness for seven months. More new birds arrive each day. It is the high tide of a far northern spring — doubly glorious and welcome because it has taken so long to get here. The birds and animals are obviously as thrilled with it all as we are. Today a mink played along a log below our bank, and muskrats swim back and forth. When they're alarmed or nervous the muskrats swim with the tail almost erect and held up out of the water. At other times they use the tail as a paddle and rudder combined. J. talks at length to one big old grandfather rat. The rat swims toward him whenever he whistles.

May 20

The other day, in the pine grove near the cabin, I met a Franklin's grouse. Instead of flying off with the usual whir and cackle, he began to advance across the soft green mosses straight toward me — in fact right up to my feet. And then he started the most magnificent courtship performance exactly two feet away. I could have leaned down and picked him up any time. He dragged his wings, spread his tail, and puffed out the bright scarlet combs over the eyes till they stood out in arcs. He pirouetted and did little demure dancing steps. And all the while the black and brown feathers on his throat and hind neck were puffed into downy balls and he was quivering and shaking and whirring in the grip of a most ardent passion. Spellbound, I watched all this for ten minutes by my watch. And finally, his ardour subsided and he stood still.

"Thank you," I cried; "that was wonderful!"

The sound of my voice reminded him suddenly that I was a lady human and not a lady grouse, a fact which, in the ecstasy of his performance, he'd apparently entirely forgotten. With a highly indignant "Tut, tut, tut, tut," he was away in a moment. A short distance off I discovered the real object of his affections high up in a young poplar tree. It was a brown female, huddled close to the trunk, and she eyed me very coldly!

Willows and alders are alive with the flashes of colour of dozens of warblers. Audubon's are the most common; such little beauties with yellow throats and topknots, blue-gray and black and white bodies. Redstarts, orange and black, northern pileolated, bright yellow with black caps, yellow warblers, canary bodies and breasts streaked with pink-brown, decorate the bushes like coloured necklaces. They are never still a second. Ruby-crowned, as well as golden-crowned, kinglets hang every dark green spruce with chains of bubbling, rippling melody. For such tiny things, only four inches long, the kinglets sing a gigantic song. Their olive-green bodies are hard to see in thick needles, but sometimes we catch a glimpse of a male, his crown perked up like a real ruby. A pair of red-breasted sapsuckers, heads, breasts, and hind necks a vivid rose, are, as they tap for grubs in branches of the willow tree, nearly the most beautiful of all.

Loons pass overhead, sounding clear, sweet, wild calls. These are the common loons whose relatives I've heard in Maine, but here they sound new notes — seldom the weird maniacal laugh. On dark storm-threatening days they give a high, ringing cry, which stirs one's blood like a bugle. The Indians say this is the call for rain; and they are right, for it's like the sudden burst of song from robins that always precedes a warm summer shower.

The lake is crowded with ducks; fighting and love-making far into the night, arriving and taking off. At evening we often count up to a hundred or more individuals on the water at this end of the lake. Dozens at a time shoot down over the cabin just at dusk, at terrific [sic] speed, with a whirring of wings and a tremendous splash as they land just below us. Sometimes they appear to miss the cabin roof by a mere two feet or so. Our days and nights resound with every variety of quawk-quawks, quata-quata-quatas, and shrill whistles. Goldeneyes, mergansers, pintails, buffleheads, baldpates; green-winged teal, scaups, gadwalls, shovelers, mallards, white-winged scoters, and ruddies; also horned and Holboell's grebes. The majority come in companies, stopping only for a rest and feed in their frantic haste to get farther north; others, which apparently nest around this region, like the mergansers, goldeneyes, buffleheads, and teal, are too busy acquiring mates and fighting rivals to have time at all for eating and sleeping.

We're catching more and more trout in the river. Beautiful fat things, eight- and ten-pounders. Most are Dollies, the pink spots on their silver bodies reminding one of the Eastern brook trout. A few, which are rather like rainbows, are the Kamloops. They have much redder flesh and taste more "fishy" than the Dollies, but we enjoy them all.

Usually Rex and I sit up on the banks watching J. I can never get over the sheer joy of just being able to sit (now that the earth is warm enough again to relax on) and do nothing but absorb and think undisturbed, but with J. near enough to make me feel safe. Several times, however, I've gone fishing too. As the river rises, the current gets stronger; landing an eight-pound fighting trout, through the hazards of swift water and floating debris, is terrific. J. shouts with glee when he's playing one and bids me sternly to be quiet. But when I hook one he yells commands in a violent manner and, no matter how mad I am, I daren't waste breath or strength at such a moment telling him so.

Most of the fish that we catch have eggs or milt in them; right now is evidently the spawning season in these parts.

Numerous whitefish congregate in the deeper pools, but these are not at all interested in bait or flies. When the Indians at Bulkley House want whitefish for food they gouge out a deep hollow in the river bed, where the stream is sluggish, and lower into it a large piece of moose meat. Later they return to the spot with forked sticks and spear the masses of whitefish which have gathered there.

Two kinds of sucker, apparently both the large- and small-scaled, are also common here and at Bear Lake. The Bear Lake Indians have told us that they use the small-scaled sucker as bait for large lake trout. The sucker is skinned carefully, stuffed with pulped deer or moose meat, and with a large hook threaded through the entire length is lowered into the lake. The line is attached to a wooden float or sealed tin can, and left overnight. In addition to lake trout, Bear Lake also gets quantities of sockeye salmon in late summer, and steelhead trout are also said to occur in the Bear River.

Minnows, no doubt one of the shiners, are everywhere in the streams and ponds around Tetana, but so far we have seen no other varieties of small fish.

May 22

Clear, blue-green Tetana has vanished. Overnight it has risen fifteen feet and become a turbulent muddy mass. The only sign that it was once clear water is where the springs come out below our bank and shoot green streaks into the dark brown. We are hard put to get good drinking water. The river has risen so high that it has backed up into the lake, so that Tetana is now "The Lake into Which the River Flows." The flood is even pouring across the willow swamp on the west in broad swift streams. Lucky for us that our cabin stands thirty feet above the usual level. Exploring new shore lines in the dugout, and avoiding being swept off in some new swift current of the flood, is a thrilling pastime. The river has become thick brown soup and we can catch no more fish. They must be hiding out in backwaters or deep pools till it clears once more. We are out of meat again and are wondering how long the floods will last. Kastberg Creek, five miles south on the trail to Takla, has become a roaring river that can no longer be crossed by man or beast.

At night the rush of mighty waters troubles our sleep. We must be cut off from Bunshaw and Bear Lake. There have been no signs of the Indians for a long time. It seems that this country is quite literally inaccessible for a large part of the year.

When I stop to consider our situation with complete candour (which somehow I now seldom do, partly because I have become accustomed to accepting it, and partly because daily thrills and drudgeries and worries are so absorbing), I think I find it even more wonderful and more awful than I had supposed. There is always that kind of heartless loveliness and ruthlessness and serene indifference to one's welfare — and yet, more and more, I'm beginning to sense what I think must be a kind of kinship with it all. There is a secure way of life, and all manner of help and care for us, if we use the wilderness rightly, study it, work with it, not against it, accept its cruelties and uglinesses with its miracles and its beauties.

Chris Czajkowski
(1947 –)

Chris Czajkowski describes herself as a child as a loner who spent thousands of hours exploring the uninhabited woods and fields behind the house "in a village in Britain." Her father was a WWII Polish refugee and the family "did not mix socially." Trained in agriculture, specifically the dairy industry, she spent time in Uganda, New Zealand and the Falkland Islands, where she worked in a sheep shearing shed. After further trips to Argentina and Chile, she emigrated to Canada. At the invitation of Trudy and Jack Turner, long-time residents in the Coast Range mountains near Bella Coola, British Columbia, she built a log cabin on Lonesome Lake near the eastern edge of Tweedsmuir Provincial Park. That cabin's construction is recorded in **Cabin at Singing River.** *She built her present cabin, located on Nuk Tessli (West Wind) Lake near Nimpo Lake, an even more remote area, without any assistance from man, woman or beast. Czajkowski is an accomplished artist and botanist as well as writer, and is preparing a work on her home called* **Diary of a Wilderness Dweller.**

Raising the Roof

from *Cabin at Singing River: Building a Home in the Wilderness* (1991)

After the stress of lumber making, cutting the roof poles seems easy. The trees that I fall are light and slim and far less terrifying than the giants I tackled last summer. As July is well advanced, the bark has loosened and they peel easily. The Turners and their horses take time out from haying to come over and haul the poles to the site.

Before starting the roof, there is one small job that has to be done — cutting a door hole. It is no longer practical to scramble over the corners of the walls as we have been doing. Experienced log builders cut the door and window holes as they erect the walls, but last summer, all I could think about were the logs; besides, I did not yet have all the window frames. These have since been gleaned in an assortment of sizes from dumps and abandoned houses; they were flown in on the same plane that had fetched my English ladies. Logic tells me that the solid, fortlike construction, which has been standing for several months now, will remain as firm as ever when I cut a hole in it, but I have the awful feeling, as the saw is poised for its long, vertical slice through the logs, that the whole structure will fall apart. It doesn't, of course. In fact, even after I have courageously cut through the logs to create the doorway, the timbers remain so tightly wedged together that it is only by using a lot of leverage with a wrecking bar and pounding with a sledgehammer that I am able to dislodge them.

I have not the slightest idea how I am going to raise the rafters and heavy purlins — the long, horizontal stringers that support the roofing; but as the Turners' barn is much higher, I know there has to be a simple method. Sure enough, Trudy, who began her apprenticeship with her father at an early age, has a solution to every problem. With a combination of skids, gin poles, peaveys and pulleys, anything can be accomplished.

In my ignorance, I assume that the roof will be finished in a couple of weeks, but it drags on for months. First, I find it alarming to be perched so high off the ground, and until a fair amount of the framework has been completed, I feel so insecure that I move only one limb at a time, like a chameleon. Second, it takes three times as long to do anything at the top of two sets of ladders. Tools are dropped or left on the ground, and precious time must be spent building scaffolding and altering it as requirements change. Third, round, not-quite-straight logs take a lot of fitting onto a not-quite-square building. And fourth, I need help more frequently. The Turners always come when they can, but they are busy with their own work — the garden and the hay — and are not always available.

Gradually, the roof takes shape. The ridgepole runs directly above the second foundation log, creating a saltbox roof with a short, steeply pitched north slope and a long, gently sloping south face which extends the full width of the house at the back but which is cut short at the front by the L. Here, I build a kneewall to fill the gap between the log walls and the roofline. From the ridgepole, I run rafters to the eaves — the extra-long timbers that cover the back south slope are particularly heavy and awkward to handle. Next come the purlins. When the porch, with its overhanging roof, is defined, the whole character of the building changes. About halfway along the north side of the roof, I position the chimney, fitting it carefully through the grid of the roof structure so that the insulated sections of stovepipe are not touching any of the timbers. Now I know exactly where to build the rock-and-concrete platform on the floor for the stove.

I like rafters to be visible from the inside of a house, so I nail the sloping ceiling on top of them, fitting the boards between the purlins. Now I discover just how uneven my hand-sawed lumber is: some boards are hump-backed and others undulate. Their edges are so irregular that all of them have to be planed to fit. But piece by piece, the sky is shut out, and the interior of the building becomes dark and gloomy. With as much trepidation as I had while cutting the doorway, I slice out two window holes to let in some light.

The salmon have started to spread across the gravel bars by the time we are ready for the roofing. As with every aspect of the house, the materials for the roof are dictated by cost and availability. Although there are plenty of cedars in the park, they cannot be touched, and there are not enough left on the property for me to emulate the Turners and make shakes. Metal roofing is beyond my pocket — all I can afford are thick rolls of tarred paper with a brown, pebbly finish. We put them on in vertical strips, preparing the narrow sections of the roof one at a time, for if the insulation gets wet, it will be ineffective. A layer of plastic goes on top of the ceiling boards, followed by batts of fibreglass; next comes another layer of boards (all tediously planed and fitted on the ground beforehand), and these are held away from the insulation by the purlins, creating a gap for ventilation. Then, a covering of building paper is laid on before the rolled roofing can finally be placed. It is heavy and stiff and easily cracks if it is cold: it can be handled only during the warm part of the day, and the sunshine hours are already short at this time of year. I fasten the rolled roofing with flat-headed nails pounded two or three inches apart along its edges. The south side of the roof has a shallow enough slope to walk on; but to nail the north side, I hang from a rope that I tied round my waist and passed over the ridge to Trudy, who belayed it around the exposed end of a rafter. The rope bites into my lower ribs, and I feel like a sack of potatoes. It takes several days to reach the halfway point and pass the chimney. That evening, Jack informs me he's heard cubs squalling and seen bear tracks beside the river. It is time to move from my camp.

I could go back to Trudy's claim cabin, but it is such an effort to haul stuff over there. It seems easier to move into the unfinished house, despite the fact that there is no floor, the wind whistles through a twelve-inch gap under the walls, the two window holes gape emptily and there is no door to hang in the doorway. This is not the triumphant entry into the complete, clean house that I have held in my mind for so long. I place a few boards on the floor joists in a back corner, and using a wheelbarrow, I relocate my camp, including the protesting cat. It is pouring with rain, and I sit on the boards in a corner of the dry half of the building, watching the water cascade through the uncovered part of the roof.

That evening, as the storm clears, the twilight gathers and the smell of home-canned beef stew (courtesy of the Turners) drifts through the gaps in the walls, a large grizzly ambles into the clearing, coming toward the house on a route his ancestors have no doubt used for centuries. I have always believed that the grizzly myth is greatly exaggerated. However, mentally sneering at other people's horror stories when there is no danger is one thing; when I am confronted with tooth and claw and flesh and blood, I am instantly terrified. My gaping, unprotected window holes suddenly seem far too big. The meaty smell of my supper will surely bring him running. What shall I do?

The dog barks. The bear stops, and a puzzled look comes over his face. "That's funny," he seems to be thinking as he stares toward the house. "Surely that wasn't here last year." Then he leisurely turns and walks, without haste, back into the forest.

The weather improves, and the roof is finished at last. The spawning is at its peak. The salmon in the river slither and sway and fight and die; the birch leaves turn golden and begin to drift toward the ground. During last year's spawning season, I saw no bears at all, but at the time, I did not realize how unusual that was. Now, I see grizzlies often as they move quietly through the forest on a game trail behind the house; they are sometimes curious but always peaceful. One sow with two cubs has become quite a fixture. She appears on the tiny island in front of my house, feeding on the white berries of the red willow. For half an hour, she pulls down the bushes and wades in the shallows, her roly-poly youngsters in tow. One cub has a dramatic white "V" on his chest, so the family is easily distinguished. I often watch them from my doorstep in the dusk.

One afternoon, I am sitting on the end of a foundation log that will eventually support my porch. It is hot, and having just eaten lunch, I am half asleep. The cat is dozing on my lap. Suddenly, she growls. I jump awake. Standing in the river is a man. He is wearing chest waders, and he carries a rifle. Unexpected visitors are pretty rare in this part of the country — we might see one or two a year; in any case, they usually come in on the trail. This man is only a few yards away from me, waist-deep in water, staring at me. The chatter of the water has disguised any sound of his approach. He sees that I have noticed him, and he waves, wading slowly toward me.

He has a companion. The two of them reach the ladder propped up against my back and rise out of the river like misplaced Tritons. I almost expect their green, shining rubber bodies to end in scaly tails.

The men are federal Fisheries officers, and every year, they walk the river to count the spawning salmon. They flew to Tenas Lake first thing this morning, and they will be picked up this evening at the lagoon. They sit on my porch and consume mugs of tea before climbing back down into the water and wading away. Instantly, the view is uninterrupted wilderness, just the singing sparkle of the river and the heavy, golden trees; I have to look twice at the tea mugs to make sure that my visitors were real.

The yellowing leaves and the smell of dying fish mean that very little good weather is left. I must work quickly to finish my shelter. I cut the remaining window holes and fit in my assortment of salvaged frames. I build a heavy door and hang it. I paint the ceiling white and try, with only partial success, to scrub the mould off the wall logs. Finally, I squeeze layers of Styrofoam insulation between the joists and start to lay the floor. My saw gives out again, and I have to solicit Jack's help to trim the final boards. Then they are all down, and suddenly, I have a house. For 18 months, this has been an idea, a dream of the future, and its completion, worked toward for so long, has crept upon me unawares. I sit in the middle of the clean, new, empty floor and marvel at it all. There are many rather drastic mistakes. The sleeping loft that covers half of the interior space is hung too low — I have to duck to walk beneath the joists. One end of the main floor is eight inches higher than the other: it is such a slope that I have had to fit the windows slightly askew to make them look right. My carpentry work around them is pretty crude, partly due to the hogbacks in the boards and partly because of my lack of patience. At the time speed seemed more important than looks. But it is a house: not just a bush cabin, but a nine-hundred-square-foot, L-shaped house. I can close the door and shut out the wind and the rain and the sound of the river; I can enjoy the warmth of the stove and cook and eat my meals in comfort.

And I have built it with my own hands.

"Grizzlies!"

It is now the end of October. Very early one morning, I load the ailing saw into my pack and head for the highway. I can see quite well in the clearing, but the darkness is impenetrable in the forest beyond the boundary fence. However, I know the way and am confident I will be able to feel the trail with my feet, something I do quite often. I walk into the blackness. Yards in front of me, a large animal explodes into action and crashes noisily through the bush. "My God! A bear!" I scoot back into the clearing and wait by the barn, heart pounding, until there is enough light to see properly. A bear it was, sure enough, for next to the trail is an anthill, dug up and ripped apart. It can only be a grizzly at this time of year: grizzlies kill and eat black bears, so the two species rarely mix. Fortunately, this grizzly was as frightened as I. It was foolish of me to travel in the dark during the spawning season.

The lagoon is still and grey, and tendrils of mist unfurl from the water like weeds. One of the great advantages of canoeing is its noiselessness. As

I slide around a clump of willows, a flock of geese erupts from the water with clamouring cries and beating wings. Behind them, through the shifting mist, stands a huge bull moose. I rest my paddle, and we watch each other. His body is blocky with autumn muscle, and a great rack of antlers spreads over his head like a coffee table. Moose and deer have no fear of boats and do not seem to associate them with humans; even when I move quite freely or speak to the dog, the bull merely lowers his head and continues his breakfast. I resume my journey, for I don't want to be caught in the dark again at the other end of the day.

A raft of cloud begins to thicken and lower, lopping off the highest points along the walls of the valley. The lake is still motionless, and fish nose pewter rings into the dark, grey-green reflections. Round the last point, cat's-paws ruffle the surface, and I suddenly hit a chilly head wind.

The stretch between the lakes is shrouded in gloom. I keep a very sharp eye out, because here, the river's multiple shallow, gravelly channels are a prime humpback-spawning area and the place is thick with bears. Just before the Stillwater, the forest ends, and the trail, half washed away, is sandwiched between a rock slide and the river. At the top of a rise, blocking the trail only 30 paces away (I measure them later), appears my second grizzly of the day. It is a big, black boar. The wind, quite strong now, is blowing directly toward me. Usually, the dog at my heels warns me if a bear is close, but this one is several feet higher than we are and its scent must be passing over our heads, for the dog is quite unaware of it. The bear and I stare at each other. The frozen moment stretches uncomfortably, and I think it expedient to look for a tree. There aren't many on the rock slide. Most of the nearest conifers have no branches for at least fifty feet, but three paces behind me, hanging over the river, is a scrubby willow. I turn and stride to it, loosening my pack. I glance at the bear. He is running toward me. Up the tree I go. The dog barks: she has sensed him at last. Another frantic look: the grizzly is galloping flat out — in the opposite direction. I am now sure that he came toward me purely out of curiosity and that when he smelled me, he could not get away fast enough. But I am unable to discuss the matter with him, and it is quite a while before my heartbeat returns to normal.

There are all sorts of theories about the do's and don'ts of bear country. Most accidents happen because the bear feels itself or its cubs are threatened; if surprise close encounters could be avoided, the risk of accident would be greatly reduced. Unfortunately, in this dark and tangled forest, it is very difficult to see the animals in time, and the constant noise of rushing water drowns out sounds that might warn either party. Many people advocate carrying a bell, reasoning that at least the bear will be forewarned, but I have yelled at bears at the top of my voice, and they have not taken the slightest bit of notice. When their heads are buried in a roaring river, far more than a gentle little tinkle is required to alert them. Besides, a bell's clanking and banging irritates me and impairs my own hearing, which I find more useful than sight in such a close environment. Smell seems to be the only thing bears really respond to.

Most bush travellers carry a rifle during spawning season, but I have never fired one and am more frightened of its misuse than I am of the grizzlies. A dog, unless it is strictly under control, can be a disaster, for if it roams loose and discovers a bear, it may run back to its owner for protection, bringing its new acquaintance with it. My dog rarely barks, and she has been trained to stay by my feet on the trail. Her nose is the best bear detector ever invented; as she is terrified of them, I can usually tell by her attitude when they are close. Her ears and tail clamp down as far as they can go, and if the bear is behind us, she walks with her head twisted over her shoulder and bumps into my legs.

However, she is obviously not infallible, and I am still trembling when I reach my canoe at the Stillwater. Despite the head wind, which is pretty strong now, I am more than glad to be away from the shore. At the foot of the lake, I start walking again, and it is not long before I see a dark figure shambling bearlike through a screen of trees. Oh no, not again! But it is only Dennis from Stuie, plodding up the trail after driving up the tote road to meet me.

I am out for a week, and during that time, the weather changes drastically. The temperature crashes to -4°F, and its subsequent rise generates a foot of snow. So the journey home is a very different one from my hike down the valley.

It is impossible to drive the tote road, because the walls of brush have been beaten down into a meshed network of branches; it is difficult enough to find a way through on foot, let alone with a vehicle. At times, the snow drags heavily at my feet, but the grizzlies have broken trail for most of the way; the length of their stride is perfect for me, and I walk quite comfortably, like Wenceslas' page, in their footprints.

There is enough current in the old river channel of the Stillwater to keep a sinuous passage open through the lake. It is strange to paddle between wide, white sheets of snow. I have started late, and the short winter day is ending. As I do not want to tackle bears in the dark, I camp under the roofed enclosure that the Turners built to house their boat at the head of the Stillwater and start up between the lakes the next morning.

There are dozens upon dozens of bear tracks of all sizes going in all directions. Many are freckled with the red duff of rotten fir, as the bears like to dig into the remains of disintegrating logs to make their beds. Although I do not see any bears this time, it is astounding to realize how many of these awesome animals make this small area their year-round home.

Hunlen Creek is an unbelievable sight. When the temperature dropped, slush ice, which stayed liquid coming down the falls, congealed upon hitting the boulder fan and flowed sluggishly like white concrete until it froze, gradually spreading over the whole area. The gullies, dry in April and torrential in June, are now completely obscured under a level white mantle. Occasionally, flowing water can be heard gurgling faintly far below. Right at the edge of the lake, buried under several feet of ice, is my canoe. Only one green tip is showing.

Fortunately, the temperature has now warmed to around freezing, and the ice is soft enough to hack away with an axe. The inside of the boat is jammed solid, and the life jacket and paddles must all be chipped free.

The sun has broken through the clouds by the time I glide into the lake, and it has become a glorious afternoon. The bluffs are yellow in the mellow light, and the snow on their ledges is dazzling against a deep blue sky. A bright network of ripple reflections wavers over the rocks along the shore; the air is sharp and sweet and very clear. Near the head of the lake, across the narrowest part, is a barrier of ice. Although it is too thin to walk on, the ice is enough to block the canoe, and I have to leave it there for the winter.

A couple of hours later, I crunch over the fields of the homestead. The deer fence wriggles like a black worm across the clearing. The sun has gone; the sky is apple green. It is already freezing hard, so it is going to be very cold tonight. My clearing looks peaceful in the evening light, for the scars of destruction have been hidden under the snow. The house with its yellow logs and smoothly blanketed roof is cozy and welcoming. Pussy Cat, as always, is pleased to see me; her fur is fluffed and crackly with cold.

I dump my pack in the middle of the empty floor and put a match to the stove. I fetch a pail of water from the river, feed the animals, light the lamp and shut the door.

I am home.

Encounters

Emily Carr
(1871 – 1945)

Emily Carr is well known as one of Canada's most famous painters whose work meditates on the nature of Canada's west coast. As well, she produced five books of stories and reminiscences, two of which, The Book of Small *(1942) and* Growing Pains *(1946), are represented in this anthology. Although Carr always kept journals, these books were written later in her life when poor health curtailed her painting. In the books, all of which are autobiographical, she recounts events charged with the heightened light of memory. The connection between nature and remembrance is an important one, for often the environment serves as a catalyst to recollecting and recapturing the past.* The Book of Small *concerns earliest events and is so named because, as the youngest child but one in the family, Carr was known as "Small."*

Green

from *Growing Pains: The Autobiography of Emily Carr* (1946)

Woods, you are very sly, picking those moments when you are quiet and off guard to reveal yourselves to us, folding us into your calm, accepting us to the sway, the rhythm of your spaces, space interwoven with the calm that rests forever in you.

For all that you stand so firmly rooted, so still, you quiver, there is movement in every leaf.

Woods you are not only a group of trees. Rather you are low space intertwined with growth.

Bless John Whiteley! Bless Algernon Talmage! the two painting masters who first pointed out to me (raw young pupil that I was) that there was coming and going among trees, that there was sunlight in shadows.

In the roof-peak of the apartment house I built was a little attic room, my favourite of all the rooms in that house.

A crooked stair led to it. The stair was in the corner of the studio. I chose this room with its wide view for my bedroom. It had low-drooped walls but the centre of the room was high. Its end walls were peaked. The naked ridge pole and studding showed, because the room was unlined. Rain pattered on the cedar shingles only a few feet above my face.

In its west-end wall the room had two large windows which appeared to be narrow because they were so high, beginning at the floor and ending right in the point of the gable. These windows let in an extensive view, a view of housetops, trees, sea, purple mountains and sky. The view seemed to come companionably into the room rather than to draw me out; and it had an additional glory, but for this glory you must look out, look down. Then you saw right into the heart of a great Western maple tree. Its huge bole culminated in wide-spread, stout branches. There was room for immense life in this bole.

The maple tree was always beautiful, always gracious. In spring it had a sunlit, pale-yellow glory, in summer it was deep, restful green, in autumn it was gold and bronze, in winter it was a gnarled network of branches. It was in winter you saw best the tree's reality, its build-up and strength.

On the whitewashed underside of the roof shingles of my attic room I painted two immense totemic Indian Eagles. Their outstretched wings covered the entire ceiling. They were brave birds, powerful of beak and talon. Their plumage was indicated in the Indian way — a few carefully studied feathers painted on wing, breast, and tail gave the impression that the bird was fully plumed.

Sleeping beneath these two strong birds, the stout Western maple tree beneath my window, is it wonder that I should have strong dreams, dreams that folded me very close!

One night I had a dream of greenery. I never attacked the painting of growing foliage quite the same after that dream I think; growing green had become something different to me.

In my dream I saw a wooded hillside, an ordinary slope such as one might see along any Western roadside, tree-covered, normal, no particular pattern or design to catch an artist's eye were he seeking subject-matter. But, in my dream that hillside suddenly lived — weighted with sap, burning green in every leaf, every scrap of it vital!

Woods, that had always meant so much to me, from that moment meant just so much more.

Louise de Kiriline Lawrence
(1894 – 1992)

For over fifty years, Louise de Kiriline Lawrence observed, banded and recorded the activities of birds in the area of her cabin near Pimisi Bay, Ontario. She was the first to study the birds of this region, and her work was recognized when she became the first Canadian woman to be voted an Elective Member of the American Ornithologists' Union. Born in Sweden and reared with Swedish royalty, she lost her first husband in the Russian Revolution and herself survived concentration camps. She emigrated to Canada and gained fame as the nurse to the Dionne Quintuplets, an experience recorded in her book The Quintuplets' First Year *(1936). She retired from nursing in 1935 and bought land on the Mattawa River, where she wrote the Dionne book in a one room log cabin. She then turned to yet another career, which grew from her interest in the bird populations around her home. During the next half-century she recorded the events of the creatures about her and produced both nature writing and scientific books and articles. She is justifiably one of Canada's most famous amateur naturalists, with seven books, seventeen scientific papers and many articles and reviews.* The Lovely and the Wild *records the realization of Lawrence's dream of living in harmony with nature. She explores the world around her and the connections between animals and humans, and the ethics involved in these relationships.*

An Exercise in Tolerance

from *The Lovely and the Wild* (1987)

I shot the red squirrel. It fell dead. A thin stream of its life's blood soaked into the ground beneath the inert form. I stared at it.

A little while ago the squirrel had tried in vain to jump to a half coconut filled with sunflower seeds. The coconut, intended strictly for the birds, was suspended from a string stretched between two trees, out of reach, I thought, of even the most enterprising squirrel. But this one was in possession of a high degree of persistency, and the frustration of not being able to achieve its goal put a resourceful twist to its endeavours. The squirrel ran up one of the trees and bit off the string. Down crashed the coconut. The squirrel squinted at the wealth of seeds spilled on the ground, ran down, and gorged itself upon the loot. This developed into a routine manoeuvre that never failed. And suddenly my patience ran out.

At that moment I took no account of my own frustration which turned into a fit of annoyance reinforced by a need for vengeance. Several things justified these feelings. First, I was interested in birds and not in squirrels and therefore the birds must be protected against the trespassing and food-stealing squirrels. Moreover, the squirrels' reputation was bad. Stealing the birds' food was only one of their minor sins. Had I not with my own eyes seen a red squirrel sitting bolt upright on a stump twirling the head of a tiny junco nestling between its front paws as if it were a nut, to the accompaniment of the junco parents' loud distress calls? And another time I heard a scream followed by ominous silence. When I got to the spot I found a pair of veeries attacking a red squirrel with a fury rarely displayed by these gentle thrushes. Why? Because the sight of the squirrel feasting upon the exposed red liver of their fledgling aroused their vehement protest, naturally. They dived at the predator, tried to unseat it, chase it, but never got close enough even to touch it. The squirrel only jumped around so that it always faced the attacking birds and continued to enjoy its ill-gotten meal.

These episodes, and also the idea acquired in childhood that the squirrels were "bad" characters, turned me against them and indeed against any other creature that was likely to interfere with those from which I reserved all my sympathy, the birds. Up to this moment I had fought the squirrels — futilely, for their desire to eat was irrepressible; unreasonably, because I never made clear to myself either their real position or mine.

What is good and what is bad? I know the answer now: all and nothing. Everything called bad may on occasion turn into a blessing and likewise all that is good can under certain circumstances become an unmitigated evil.

Suddenly the iniquity of my deed struck me full force. The squirrel was without fault, an innocent. Naturally the thwarted urge to eat moved it to do just what it did, an act of distinct survival value no matter how the animal arrived at doing it. Persistency and the energy that fires it are among life's most significant ingredients. Their suppression often destroys success. And everybody, even a red squirrel, is entitled to his own measure of success. The red squirrel had merely followed a true and logical tendency and for this reason alone was worthy of my whole-hearted approval instead of extinction.

Disturbing thoughts! Stupidity and injustice are uncomfortable terms when applied to one's own mistakes. Prejudice is a dreadful hindrance in any endeavour to acquire realistic understanding. But this was the goal I had set myself long ago. The inept idea of dividing nature into parts — these are the good ones and those are the bad ones, some to be overly indulged and others disliked, disdained, persecuted — was a greatly confusing stumbling block.

Naturally the realization of all this did not come overnight, but the incident was a turning point. Many relapses impeded progress. But at least I understood now that the inclination to kill was wrong. Drastically and thoughtlessly I had played with the life and death of creatures that lived around us and had no means of defense except their utter innocence. But to dissipate the confusions of which I was guilty required a deeper penetration into the problems of predators and prey, of life and death, devoid of sentimentality. A prolonged effort was needed to learn about the lives and the requirements and the reactions of these "bad" characters, the red squirrels in particular. And in the account of my endeavours along these lines I shall use Kicki, an irresistible female squirrel, as the prototype who will represent all the red squirrels I have ever known. She was in fact the Red Queen of another Wonderland, who metaphorically took me by the hand and introduced me to many phases of the red squirrels' remarkable and intimate world.

How the rapprochement between Kicki and me started I cannot remember. It was probably just one of those things that happen, based on the subtle attraction that develops occasionally between two characters whose reactions to each other are more favourable than otherwise. For my part I wanted to be friends with Kicki in order to learn at first hand what it was like to be a red squirrel. That I stooped to employ artificial aids in attaining this objective may be forgiven on the premise that the goal justified the means in mutual measure. My lard pudding, a concoction of rolled oats, fat, and water, was and is a delicacy universally approved by all the animals of our forest from the black bears to the chipping sparrows. A small chunk of it, named a courtesy ball, wrecked many a barrier of fear and distrust erected between man and beast since the days of the lost Paradise.

As for Kicki, the beginnings were too casual to suggest any feelings for or against. She took me in her stride as she would the next tree on her arboreal highways. But because dash and boldness were features infused from birth into her character, she left herself open to such insinuating things as courtesy balls and me.

Being a typical representative of the red squirrel tribe, Kicki differs from the common throng only in that each of her distinctive traits is etched with reinforced emphasis. There are no two ways about anything she does. The situation that stimulates her into action makes her perform exactly according to the true need of the moment. Although moods and external circumstances often influence her responses and lend to them a variety of nuances, the results are by and large never out of line, depending of course on the standpoint from which they are judged.

Kicki's whole life and being is dominated by nervous tension that expresses itself particularly well in the movements of her bushy tail and in her vocal contributions. Her large eyes, that seem never to blink and whose prominence is somewhat enhanced by a ring of small light-coloured hairs, give the impression of a slightly overactive thyroid. Yet with all her amazing vitality she is an expert at snatching catnaps at the most unlikely moments. She just stops and naps, then and there, for a few seconds or a minute or two, ample allowance, apparently, for restoking her energy. Only in the privacy of her snug nests and hideouts does she give herself up to sleep with the same consummate abandon with which she pursues action during her waking hours.

Her days are filled to the brim with important business that carries her through the year with zest. After she finishes rearing her young during spring and summer, she begins hoarding for the winter. After this is completed, she goes on to build or to refurbish her winter nest, a bulky affair tucked into a bushy conifer that stands in a sheltered place. She constructs the nest for the most part of dead leaves tied together with strips of cedar bark. During the winter she keeps alive on her hoarded goods, supplemented by buds of spruce and fir and whatever the feeding station has to offer. Finally, after some ado, she accepts a father for her prospective young and goes to work preparing the nest for the happy event. At this juncture she loses all interest in dalliance and arbitrarily dissolves the ties with the father, at least temporarily.

I have the greatest respect and admiration for Kicki as a mother. She usually houses her babies in an abandoned nesthole or a knothole in the trees high up away from terrestrial dangers. Latterly she moved into a new apartment under the eaves of the porch, in the space formed by the overhang of the roof and the boards enclosing the ends of the rafters. Through a narrow aperture between the wall and the boards she squeezes in and out. She lines the nest with dead grasses, straws, strips of cedar bark, bits of tissue paper, and hairs from her moulted winter coat, to make a snug bed for each new litter. To facilitate transportation she manipulates the stuff with her dextrous front paws into tiny balls which she carries home in her mouth.

By early May motherhood imprints itself upon her whole being. She looks dishevelled and worn from the strain of nursing. Often there is an expression upon her face — or so I fancy — as if the blessings of motherhood were not quite what they are made out to be and hence should be compensated by a more generous distribution of courtesy balls. Anyhow this is the way she acts, although naturally the nourishment the babies drain from her requires replacement by measure. Later on, as the period of weaning begins, she quickly recuperates.

All through this time Kicki remains strictly and efficiently vigilant. She allows neither outsiders nor babies any liberties. Once during play one of her kits took an awful tumble through the slit entrance of the eaves nest down into the rosebush and then scampered off to hide among the lilies, none the worse but scared to death. Upon hearing its whimpers of dire loneliness, Kicki rushed to its aid. Instantly locating the youngster, she grasped it by the scruff of the neck and carried the now perfectly limp and silent burden up on the telephone wire beside the eaves. Precariously balancing herself and the baby on this trembling support, she proceeded to squeeze and push, push and squeeze the child through the narrow cranny to safety, an awkward and acrobatic feat few mothers could have performed.

In due time she literally shakes off motherhood with the same perfect sense of timing as she entered upon it. Under her nose, so to speak, now appear fruits, berries, and other growth in such profusion that all cannot be eaten at once. When wealth of one kind or another overwhelms her, a strong inclination always directs her to tuck away into any convenient shelf or cranny what she cannot makes use of at once. Thus, driven by this urge to pluck the lot, she begins hoarding.

Though it is still only late summer and ample time is left before the first snowfall, she is suddenly possessed by frantic haste. Toadstools begin wandering through the undergrowth, seemingly on their own, with Kicki hidden under their top hats, laboriously propelling them. She races up the trunks of the evergreens and nips off the cones, one by one. She races down, picks up the fallen cones, and runs off with them, tips first. If she carried them in any other way, she would never get them through the narrow corridor to her selected cache. With her face a sticky mess of gum, she works from dawn to nightfall, allowing herself scarcely enough recess to feed and to rest.

Just how strong the urgency to hoard is in a squirrel, Kicki ably demonstrated one year when because of a drought nothing except clusters of small brown cedar cones hung on the trees and the toadstool harvest failed. First she stripped all the cones off the cedars. Then, when she could not find anything else to hoard, she collected small rocks. In ardent pursuit of her seasonal task she ran with the stones in her mouth, every so often dropping them because they were heavy and awkward to carry. She picked them up again and then carried them, jumpety-hop, over rocks and other obstacles, through the tall bracken, to her storeroom, with the same enthusiasm as if they were cones. In the winter she gave no inkling of being put out by her "bread" having turned to stone. Judging by the alley of tracks her feet wore in the snow from the feeding station to the cache under the balsam fir, it may be presumed that she felt no pinch at all and as usual rode the crest of the wave in her own indomitable style.

Kicki arranged her caches in a variety of places, under tree roots, under rocks, in unused holes dug by other animals. Once she took possession of our cellar, to which she gained entrance through an unscreened ventilator. The stores she amassed here defy either count or description. Presumably, the proportion of the space she found at her disposal under our floors induced her to go far beyond her usual limits and needs, with respect both to the volume and to the time she allotted to her harvesting. On another occasion she dropped a large supply of spruce cones into the shallow never-freezing water of the spring's overflow. In February she dug a tunnel through the snow to this cache and presently came up with one fresh cone after the other. In a strip of sunshine at the base of a tall poplar she sat down, picked off all the scales, and devoured the seeds with relish.

Sometimes, as I watched her, instead of running off with her load to her storeroom she hastily buried it at random. With quick paws she dug a little hole, put the stuff down, patted it into place, then covered it at arm's length. Apparently these extracurricular burials stemmed from her strong reluctance to go directly to the cache while she was being watched. In fact she merely disposed of her load quickly and conveniently; in effect her performance distracted my attention and kept the location of her head office secret and safe. But she never revealed whether she came back for the buried store or merely forgot all about it.

Kicki possesses a keen sense of ownership of the space surrounding her nursery, her winter chambers, her caches, and other special places. She claims these spaces simply by being there and supports her title to them in various ways. There she lives, although more than once I have met her quite far beyond the more or less staked out limits of her domains. On the ground as well as in the trees she established habitual roads and avenues for her own convenience. Habit is for her — as well as for me — a great boon to existence. Indeed, some of these trails of hers on terra firma actually come to appear worn from the repeated passage of her pattering feet.

In defense of her territory, Kicki treats trespassing members of her own species most harshly. In fact, especially during the periods of her annual cycle when her possessive urges reach a peak, she hardly tolerates another red squirrel on the premises. These peaks generally coincide with times of greatest activity that are also times of greatest stress — for instance, when she is nursing her young, at the height of the hoarding season, and in winter when food is scarce and keeping alive is a major business. This aggressiveness is natural and it is a true tendency. The rejection of interference when the demands of self-preservation need to be met is not antisocial behaviour but fully justified. On these occasions the individual triumphs over the group, and in the end it is the individual that maintains the species.

The incitement to hostilities works on Kicki by degrees and is brought to a culmination by means of a set sequence of actions. There is no question of deviation from this pattern of behaviour; only the speed with which the climax is produced depends on the situation and the particular way that the intruder's approach plays upon her responses at the given moment. Four main stages of stereotyped actions bring her into a fighting mood: pseudo-mastication, loud chatter, drumming with the hind legs and, finally, explosive chatter.

By studying the variations in speed and intensity with which these actions are performed, one can easily tell exactly how the squirrel feels and what is going to happen next. The mastication is a chewing motion with nothing in the mouth, pure pretence, similar to the way old people sometimes chew when they get excited and cannot control their chins. Birds, and other animals, too, resort to the same trick at a time when their ire is aroused but their response as yet fails to be crystallized into decisive action because the situation kindles too complex a range of reactions.

With the loud chatter Kicki proclaims that she is getting bolder. "I'm master here, get out," the expression on her face seems to say. Impatiently she drums her hind legs. Hares and rabbits also drum with their hind legs loudly and suddenly, and so startling is this sound that the pursuing enemy is often stopped in his tracks for an instant, the precious instant that gives the pursued a breathless chance of escape. The hare is frightened out of its wits and the next second flees like the wind, zigzagging wildly to throw the enemy off scent, off balance, anything to gain a foot of distance between them. Kicki's drumming, by contrast, contains more pugnacity than the hare's and indicates that she is getting really angry and means it. She emphasizes the threat by bursting into explosive chatter, a kind of staccato rapid-fire performance uttered with such passion that she actually shakes from emotion and her tail twitches eloquently.

In all these preliminaries an intimate interaction develops between her own and the opponent's reactions, a process within each that alternatively oscillates between urges of prudence and audacity. This wards off actual combat and directs their next moves. At this point the whole affair usually dissolves, with Kicki discreetly being left in undisputed control of her domain. But, if not, like a dwarf demon on the rampage, Kicki flings hesitation to the winds and dashes at her adversary. Spiralling up and down the tree trunks after her foe, leaping cross-country in high style, she finally throws herself bodily at the interloper. The impact upsets the other and the two roll together as one ball of fur, hissing, spitting, clawing, biting.

Sometimes when Kicki happens to be surprised at close quarters while having dinner at the squirrel plate, she reacts full throttle. Her tail twitches violently, she screams. This scares and enrages the rival. As the latter moves to counter her challenge, Kicki rises upon her hind legs to her full height, looking like a miniature bear ready for the devastating embrace. In rhythmic hops she advances and the usual melee results, with moves faster than the eye can follow, leaving in the end a few drops of red blood spattered over the battle scene.

Her relations with other animals Kicki handles with consummate plasticity. At such encounters experience influences her approach and so do the size and temper of the intruder.

I do not know which one, Kicki or the beautiful white ermine as it enters the squirrel's domain, ought to be judged the most fierce. Lithe and inimitably graceful, the weasel in winter dress with its eyes shining like beads and the black-tipped tail bringing the elongated white body to an elegant end emerges from a snow tunnel dug by the squirrel. It dashes quickly hither and yon in a seemingly haphazard search for titbits, finds one, dashes back out of sight. Out it comes again, tugs at a piece of chicken carcass too big for the tunnel entrance, pulls it asides, stops, listens, looks — intent, utterly alert, its triangular face raised on a strong muscular neck overemphasized in size as compared with the slenderness of the rest of its body. Now Kicki catches sight of it. Both dash into the same tunnel — and I sit tense waiting for the signs of the bloody drama that surely is taking place inside. But the next instant the squirrel shoots out of the tunnel, all in one piece, and the weasel peeps forth and observes the scenery with a perfectly innocent look on its face. Suddenly, the two tear at each other again. They fight in the opening of the tunnels, like cats, never touching each other, but with sparks of temper and fury flying, a seesawing battle, each alternatively attacking with reckless daring and withdrawing bristling, ears flattened, teeth gleaming. They are so evenly matched that nothing whatever comes of the encounter and it dissolves harmlessly.

The only leporine inhabitant of our forest is the snowshoe hare. It is almost one and a half times as large as the red squirrel. In the spring Old Doe leaves the swamp where she usually winters and takes up residence in the neighbourhood of our house. There she and her families, one or two, sometimes three, a year, stay around until late fall. Some years there are more of them, in other years many fewer hares go back to the swamps for the winter. This fluctuation in the hare population usually repeats itself every ten years or so. The ones we have known personally have as a rule survived about four or five years.

Since we got grass to grow on the rocks around the house Old Doe has been very happy. In the early morning when the dew is on the green grass she loves to sit with all four feet gathered under her and eat her fill. Faithful to the habit of most of the forest's denizens, she rests during the forenoon. About the middle of the afternoon she emerges to spend the best part of her day abroad, eating, hopping around, sometimes engaging in various social activities when the demands of her progeny in the hollow under the great log leave her some free time. In the night she takes another period of rest. In the lives of all animals, this wonderfully appropriate division of the twenty-four hours into rhythmic alternations between action and quiescence, if left undisturbed, effectively contributes to their well-being and keeps them in top condition.

Old Doe is also very fond of bread and rolled oats — and so is Kicki. This therefore is the medium that quite frequently brings these two together. When Kicki finds Old Doe enthroned upon one of her favourite feeding spots she first essays intimidation and races madly to and fro in front of the hare's twitching nose. This startles and confuses Old Doe. With all four feet off the ground at the same time she leaps away from the source of irritation, leaving the field open to Kicki who loses not a second in supplanting her on the disputed site. There she sits chattering away, making lightning turns always to face the hare just in case Old Doe might sneak an attack upon her. But even a hare's timidity has its limits. Quite often Old Doe elects to stand her ground and she imparts this decision by snapping at Kicki. In the face of such odds the red fury can do little else than beat a strategic retreat, though never without her usual bounce.

One might expect that the deer's intrusion upon Kicki's premises would set her back on her heels. But nothing of the sort happens. For the most part Kicki ignores the deer and the deer take scant notice of the small fry of the forest. This is the safest, and there is really sufficient room for them all. Their food requirements, their modes of living are different and thus create no conflict of interests. Yet the crossing of their paths at the feeding station brings them within the critical distance of each other. With unparalleled nerve Kicki begins to run in figure eights in and out between the legs of the towering ruminants, an ingratiating manoeuvre, an incongruous and anomalous invitation to play on Kicki's part, plainly exposing the mixture of feelings that possesses her, fright, daring, appeasement. Konrad Lorenz, the famous student of animal behaviour, gives an account of a small puppy's behaving in exactly the same way at its first meeting with a very large black dog.

Startled at first, the deer become slightly skittish. But Kicki is too nimble to fall foul of their hoofs. As all animal-watchers well know, the abnormally large provocation is apt to elicit the anticlimactic reaction. Just this is what happens to Kicki. She stops, sits up in front of the deer. Holding her stomach tight with her front paws, she tests the air with her sensitive nose. With prettily cocked ears Goliath looks down upon David. For a long instant, both of them trembling lightly with arrested excitement, the two touch noses. The secret communication satisfies. The deer resumes browsing and the squirrel runs off.

Mute communications of this kind exchanged at unscheduled meetings between the most unlikely participants are not at all uncommon. With her pouches full Shortytail, the chipmunk, runs in great haste on the way to her hideout. Suddenly she comes face to face with the flicker which is picking ants on the slope in front of the house. Startled by the unexpected and close encounter — the chipmunk almost ran into the flicker — both freeze motionless. Then, a little gingerly but without hurry or hostility, the chipmunk's nose meets the bill of the flicker. That is enough. Without further ado each resumes his, her, previous occupation.

These episodes are good examples of nature's manifold ways of avoiding wasteful conflict. It is of special interest that the absence of disturbing factors, which are apt to increase nervous tension and often bring about distorted and exaggerated responses, quite commonly favours the adjustments necessary for peaceful contact between animals in the wild, whose relations may not under all circumstances be quite so benevolent.

Kicki's associations with birds are a matter of some delicacy and quite different from her rapport with other animals. Generally speaking, the red squirrel is a vegetarian whose favourite foods include nuts, seeds, mushrooms, fruits, and berries. Comparatively rarely, because the season is limited, the squirrel eats the eggs and the young of birds; under certain circumstances involving intense nervous tension, it may attack and kill adult birds.

In the first case, the number of nests that the squirrel misses during a season is quite astonishing. This, of course, also depends on circumstances and may vary greatly in different localities. Part of the reason for this is the squirrel's inclination to keep to its own most travelled trails. Nests situated off these routes enjoy a certain immunity. But when the squirrel finds a nest, nothing stops it from picking it clean, one by one, of eggs or young. The squirrel's persistency, even against great odds, is legendary. On occasion the little animal's fine nose detects the edible contents behind the wall of the gourdlike cavity belonging to a hole-nesting bird. Should the parent bird bar the entrance and in this strategically safe position use its bill in effective defense, the frustrated squirrel attacks the wall itself and attempts to break an entry. Only the solidness of the wood coupled with the sustained vigilance of the parent birds safeguards from the squirrel's wildly tearing teeth whatever lies at the bottom of the nest cavity.

I have never known an instance of true predation by a squirrel upon an adult bird, but a squirrel may attack a bird under special provocation or in abnormal situations. The banding cages, if not closely watched, may on rare occasions prove a deathtrap for a luckless bird caught with a squirrel near or actually in the trap with the bird. Sudden loss of freedom causes a bird to panic. Fright sometimes kills outright. Fright expressed by wild movements — a bird's beating wings and its reckless efforts to get out — is contagious. This throws the squirrel entirely out of character and, unless the panic stops as the hapless bird quickly finds an opening for escape, in the twinkling of an eye the squirrel is a killer. The skunk's, the weasel's, the racoon's traditional ravages in the farmer's chicken house may often enough be the result of similar tension-producing situations, when the animal's natural snooping predacity traps it inside with a mob of dangerously panic-stricken birds. The word for the madness that affects the killers is therefore neither ferocity nor voracity, but fright.

Otherwise Kicki harbours no malevolence toward the birds, though her innate aggressiveness leads her always to insist on dominating the scene. She allows no frivolities and she acts accordingly whenever the situation demands it, by making short runs or sudden jumps at the birds to keep them in line. Only the crows and the blue jays occasionally turn the tables on the squirrel. They, and the barred owl, are the only birds I know that can outwit a red squirrel. All of them use the same technique: persistent pursuit accompanied by wing-flapping. The last is the essential part of the ritual that usually assures the pursuer's success. Its effect upon the squirrel is confusion at first, but this rapidly changes to fright and then to panic, and with that complete disarmament. With respect to the crows and the blue jays, the issue is never more serious than the squirrel's loss of a courtesy ball or a piece of suet, which the birds espy as it is being carried away and covet. But when the owl is on the scene, the life of the squirrel is in the balance. By a series of manoeuvres that often seem awkward and aimless, the owl works the squirrel into a state of abject distraction by driving it into places, out on branches, into corners, where it must backtrack or take inordinate risks. Sooner or later the inevitable happens. This is one game that the red squirrel rarely or never wins.

What exactly caused our neighbourhood animals suddenly to indulge in exaggerated and often destructive behaviour was for a long time a puzzling problem. That frustration played a large part was not difficult to divine. An unusually successful breeding season, bringing about a serious temporary overcrowding of squirrels and other small animals, as a natural consequence gave rise to overly intense competition. The effect of these circumstances did not come to light until an interesting state of affairs developed quite by chance, resulting from changes I made in the set-up of the feeding station.

By this time the elimination, either by shooting or displacement, of any animal whose behaviour interfered with our purposes in some way had long since been rejected. Displacement, which at first seemed a humane substitution for the gun, was abandoned after two of the displaced animals, a red squirrel and a young woodchuck, gave indications that this was not true. The red squirrel returned within a week, but the young woodchuck, which had started homeward upon release and kept oriented in the right direction for over an hour, did not make it. Obviously neither animal tolerated the displacement. The gamut of unknown and frightening dangers these little beasts had to run in entirely strange surroundings is not difficult to imagine. Familiarity with its environment, the knowledge of where the good hiding places are in an emergency, may spell the difference between life and death. And previous experience with neighbours and other occupants of the land must give an animal, if not a sense of security, at least a far better chance of escaping dangers than an altogether unknown place can provide. Hence displacement is a hardly less drastic measure to impose upon an animal than sudden death.

Other measures, therefore, had to be devised to counteract the obviously rising tensions and I tried rearrangements at the feeding station. To start with I separated the feeding places. I figured that if each animal could be persuaded to find its food in a certain place without having to endure too much interference from the others, a great deal of frustration might be avoided. So the bird-feeders were made squirrel proof by means of shields, upside-down funnels. The squirrels got their daily rations served on special easily accessible plates. Old Doe was persuaded to look for bread and grain on certain rocks — that is, until the squirrels and chipmunks got wind of this, although despite clashes complaisant sharing between them and the hare was not unusual. Finally, the racoons and the skunks got their own dishes too. Fortunately they did not all feed at the same time of the day.

Everything worked well until competition reached what seemed to be a critical level. Being the most highly strung of the lot, the squirrels showed the effects of the situation most seriously. Among them were five whose reactions were remarkably different from one another.

Squirrel 1 was by nature an aggressive female of Kicki's type. The squirrel proof feeder affronted her. With unrelenting tenacity, day by day, she concentrated her efforts upon its conquest, running up the post and into the funnel. In her frustration at never getting any farther she compensated by establishing her own special territory around the post and opposing the approach of everyone, her own kind in particular, with exaggerated fury. Erect upon her hind legs she would advance upon the intruder in jerky hops and with front paws held like those of a boxer about to deal the knock-out blow, she would fling herself at him, screaming at the top of her voice. With each thwarted attempt to scale the feeder, the quicker and more violent were her attacks. She went completely crazy, mercilessly attacked Old Doe as she passed by in all innocence, clawed at our feet, snarling, whenever we came within a certain distance of the feeder — certainly a most interesting example of how irritation beyond endurance can sometimes explode into exaggerated and irrelevant behaviour.

The squirrel-proof feeder also jarred the nerves of Squirrel 2. But, unlike the first, this one did not try to conquer it. Instead the little animal relieved its frustration by digging holes in the ground below the feeder, small neat holes, dozens of them, at distances of a few inches to two feet from the feeder post. It is well known that animals, including man, under stress often perform acts quite unrelated to the situation at hand, and the so-called "sparking-over" activity is an important ingredient in the process of dissipating the effects of stress.

Squirrel 3 found her way into the house by chance one day when the door was open. There she discovered the place where I kept the courtesy balls, and from then on she slipped in whenever the door was ajar. Later, when she found the door closed, she adroitly learned to push in one of the window screens. Thereupon she loped around the table, picked up a ball, perched on the back of a chair, and proceeded to feast upon it. The remarkable deliberation with which she performed all these actions set her behaviour in sharp contrast with that of the other four squirrels, and her easy adaptability thus furnished her with an outlet whereby she avoided frustration.

Squirrel 4 was much more highly strung and as a result she reacted with greater intensity. Instead of approaching me with confidence to receive her courtesy ball as she had done up to then, she stretched out full length along the ground, her hind legs spread-eagled behind her, her tail with its tip quivering curved tightly over her back and head. In this highly exaggerated pose she crawled to my hand. When I was not there to serve her, she attacked the house. Frantically she gnawed at the window frame, at the sill, at the door. She made a dreadful mess of all three. Whenever possible I tried to forestall her by offering her the prize she was after. But — and this is the most interesting part of the story — if the door was open and she could easily have slipped in to get what she wanted, she seemed entirely unaware of the opportunity. She gnawed at the open door with the same frenzy as when she found it closed. The passion with which she performed this activity nevertheless gradually dispelled her built-up nervous tension.

When I first knew her, Squirrel 5 was certainly not vicious by nature. But she reacted to the stress-filled situation and the strong competition in a way that made her vicious in act. Earlier, when she had mistaken the tip of my finger for a courtesy ball, which happened at times, she had merely closed her teeth on it gently and released it. Now she snapped, and as stress in creased she snapped more viciously, drawing blood. Under pressure her behaviour degenerated still further. She began to molest the birds and whenever she succeeded in cornering one she was apt to kill it. It became a habit, a true case of the blooded tooth and nail. She caught one downy woodpecker in one of the banding traps, killed it, and then ran away as if she had nipped off a cone and let it drop. She went for another woodpecker, but that time I saw her and stopped the murder. She was a sorely stress-ridden creature but not a killer in the true sense.

The whole situation got more and more out of hand. Hot mustard and a strong solution of mothballs painted on the woodwork of the window and the door partially discouraged the destructiveness of Squirrel 4; closing all the traps and eliminating other places where the birds could get caught by the chasing squirrel staved off the killer tendencies of no. 5. But neither preventive was foolproof.

Then, finally, almost imperceptibly, things began to change. What happened? Only this: autumn changed into winter. The animals that could not find sufficient food from the forest and the feeding station drifted away, others vanished for unknown reasons, leaving conditions in a state of greater stability and balance, where life still caused stress but in other ways and to a somewhat lesser degree.

Nervous tension that builds up under stress seems to be one of the most vital instruments in nature's self-regulatory systems. It tends to direct the living creature into channels of behaviour that in the strangest ways counteract upsetting pressures created in the course of existence and thus ultimately subserve the restoration of harmonious balance.

I never knew the exact time of Kicki's disappearance. In some way it was eclipsed by the presence of another squirrel, one just as alert and aggressive as she was, one pervaded with the same amount of nervous energy as she always possessed, one who, according to law and order, filled the empty space so that there was no loss.

Peri McQuay
(1945 –)

"On a Morning so Beautiful it Makes a Mockery of Fear" won the 1992 Fiddlehead *award for best wilderness writing. It is now included in* A Wing in the Door, *a memoir of the rehabilitation and release of a red-tailed hawk christened Merak. The book, as well as the essay, investigates the ambiguous and shifting boundaries between the human and animal worlds and captures the uncertain border between fear and friendship. Peri McQuay is also the author of a collection of essays about rural life,* The View from Foley Mountain *(1987), and is preparing another work,* A Foley Mountain Book of Days. *Her essay on the genre of nature writing is also included in this anthology.*

On a Morning so Beautiful
it Makes a Mockery of Fear

from A Wing in the Door:
Adventures with a Red-Tailed Hawk (1993)

On this May morning I scarcely shrug when I find the power off. Instead, I take it as a sign that I am not meant to be working. And so I walk out, just as I am, long skirt, bare legs, ridiculous old straw sunhat. At first, slightly guilty about the unearned holiday, I stay close to home, listening to the birds — the flicker, rose-breasted grosbeaks, the wren's fountain of song. I pry in the garden, joyfully discovering the latest upthrusting shoots — lilies, colchicum, bellflower. For a long while I stand basking in the thrum of my honeybees, watching their shadows cross their dooryard board on their way in to the hive, their leg baskets laden with pollen colours too numerous to single out. The surrounding wild cherry blossoms are alive with bees. For the first time this spring I can hear my "bee-loud glade" once again. Now, with the slightest stirring of a breeze, the small cherry petals begin to drift down in confetti-like swirls.

In the beginning I am content to loiter close to home. But watching the rain of petals makes me want to see the old orchard behind the house, now at the peak of its blossom. After this spring's heavy rains, the half-wild field is still sodden and difficult to walk, especially as I am neither dressed nor shod for rough walking. But there is a mesmerizing charm to the May morning which draws me on. Even before I can hear the bees in the largest of the old apple trees, I can smell the apple blossoms' rose-like scent. And indeed, everywhere I walk on this day, the trees' auras are very palpable.

The air is heavy, fragrant with all the tree blossoms of my world, languorous, weighted down by a searching sun, as yet unscreened by summer leaf-shade. Yet in spite of the unseasonable heat, I decide to continue on, past the orchard and across the field to a whaleback of rocks which I discovered last autumn. In the heat and sun there is an unmistakable feeling of growth rushing ahead. The mouse-ear oak leaves are swelling, and the oak trees themselves are sending forth lime-green tassels. I squelch up the field, past the unnaturally bushy and solitary field pine and, at the forest at the field's end, turn into a laneway. Here I am discouraged to find flourishing more poison ivy than ever before.

Now set on my course, however, I unroll my socks and, tugging them up my bare legs for protection, walk on. The heat, the last lingering blackflies, the poison ivy to be avoided, and the heavy, wet walking steal away some of the day's charm. For all the spring beauty, though, I feel drawn to continue. There is a strong sense that I am walking away from the house's artificiality towards truth.

Usually when I reach the long stretch of granite, I sit for a while, brooding over the lacy green lichens which halo the pink rocks, but today the searching brightness of approaching noon robs the granite of much of its colour. I will not linger here as I had planned to. However, heat-dazed as I am, I feel unable to stop walking. I will just go past the rocks before I turn back, I promise myself. It will be a good chance to see if there might be wild orchids in bloom in the queer gully beyond. Last fall I often thought the place seemed perfect for them. A small pine grove, it has acid soil, sphagnum moss tentacles everywhere, and ground cedar plantations under pines. But this morning I am disappointed. The only flowers I can find are the slight candles of Canada mayflowers and, in the heavy shade, these are still not fully out.

Then, as I kneel on a dense cushion of moss to investigate, there is a burst, followed by a stamping and clattering. A doe plunges away through the trees, her long white tail flashing an alarm. As always, I am rueful that my intrusion has sent the deer off, and sorry also that I have been unable to see her better. Now, I wish I had remained sitting on the rocks. If I had, the deer might slowly have revealed herself to me, unafraid and natural.

Although I have missed my chance with the doe, I am sufficiently aroused by her startling exit to want to keep going. I decide to push on out of the pine thicket and along a well-worn animal trail which leads to a small, secluded pond. Possibly I might sight the bittern I have heard "glunking" back that way. Out once again walking in a heavy field and under the breathless sun, not surprisingly, I do not find the bittern. After all, I reflect, his booming call generally comes in the early evening. Instead, a host of redwings shrill their "oka-lee's," guarding their nests in the cattails by the pond.

Idly, I follow a chain of rocks extending through clumps of willows into the heart of the pond. Standing at the tip of this rocky peninsula, I bend to pick up a freshly cut maple sapling, its keys still hanging from its branches, and shake my head over the surge of beaver which has led to the recent exploitation of even pitiful little pools such as this.

Suddenly and nearby, I hear a startling, coughing scream. The sound has some of the quality of the howling bark of foxes, scouring the fields on moonlit nights. Yet, and there it is again, and then once again, there is a difference. While sounding utterly ruthless, like a primitive violence howling out of the earth itself, the foxes' calls have always been steady and decisive. Their use is to startle prey and to keep in contact while searching our fields. But in these sounds that I am hearing now, there is a note of panic and uncertainty that is almost a vomit of noise. My wandering mind is jolted short as I understand the dangerous proximity of the cries. At the same moment, I see a broad flash of reddish brown. It is the doe, stalking restlessly at the edge of the pine grove. Now I recognize that, by following the deer trail out onto this peninsula, I have effectively cut myself off from escape.

The menacing, and I am beginning to be aware of just how menacing, calls surely are being given by the doe which had dashed past me. Either she is preparing to give birth, or (and far more likely) she is defending new-born fawns that must be hidden in a glade all too near me. In either case I am realizing that the actions of what normally would be a timid, furtive creature, now not only will be totally unpredictable but also may well be dangerous. Except for the first warning flash, I have not even seen my foe. She is there; she is not there. I have only my ears to grope with if I am to know my adversary at all.

This time I am truly trapped. The only obvious escape route would have me return by the trail, immediately past the deer. It's true that she has retreated to the thicket again, but her howls are increasing in frequency and agitation. Never before on my walks have I let myself get in a position where I could not safely get out. In the midday heat, there is an unreal quality which keeps me from confronting the very real danger I am in. The blackbirds continue to sing; nothing has changed except for the doe, who now is silent again. Did I imagine the menace? On such a morning surely nothing dangerous could happen? Is this how a mesmerized rabbit feels when she is confronted with a stalking fox? My eyes dart, trying to consider possibilities. On three sides I am surrounded by brackish, weed-filled pond; it would be virtually impossible to swim away from the doe's territory. Even if the pond were shallower than it appears, its bottom surely would be too treacherously soft for walking; anyhow, the very thought is disgusting.

But the danger is real; I cannot afford disgust. The deer's trumpets are renewed and are coming closer. I will have to do something to protect myself right away. Then maybe I can consider how I am going to escape. There are no trees sturdy enough to climb, and even if there were, they would only offer a temporary solution. I have to keep reminding myself that this deer will not be leaving in time. She has an urgent need to protect her nursery. Still dazed by heat and disbelief, my first instinctive act is to snatch up a large branch that I could brandish, if necessary. But alas, the only branch that comes to hand is a rotten piece of old fence-rail. It might add stature to my waving arms, if I were desperate, but certainly would crumple if I were forced as a last resort to use it to drive the deer away from me.

And so I stand, profoundly alone, on a morning so beautiful it makes a mockery of the fear and menace confronting me. A strong sense tells me to wait it out. A sneaking wildness within suggests that I would gain from the experience. If I sat quietly on the shore of the pond for a few hours, surely the doe would become calm and go about her business, letting me see her fawns. But a commoner sense warns that in this situation time would not help. Sooner or later I must cross that nursery and this surely would renew the deer's savage panic.

The increasing bellows, ever bringing the unseen deer circling closer, tell me that I should be taking the threat seriously. I will have to investigate other escape routes, however difficult they might be. My first thought is a deer trail leading away from the thicket, but down through heavy shrubs into a muddy, wet tunnel that is only waist high. It would be useless: to pass through I would have to crawl, and if the doe were to follow me I would be hopelessly outmatched. Looking over the willows and across the pond, I know that beyond the boggy area surrounding me there must be what I hope will be a safely distant field with a sheltering corridor of tall spruces.

So, drawing on long-forgotten childhood stalking skills, I begin cautiously advancing my feet across the marsh grass from hummock to hummock, sometimes using my rotten fence-rail as a balancing pole, some-times clinging to the dense marsh shrubs, conscious that if the panicky deer were to attack, I have worsened my position. It would be impossible either to keep my balance or to jump and wave my arms as I had earlier thought of doing. Another howl, closer yet. In order to get beyond the nursery to the open field, while avoiding the turbid water at the pond's centre, I discover that I first will have to parallel the doe's grove, actually approaching her territory.

And at long last the phantom appears across the pond. Her red sides steamy and heaving, she is stamping and snorting, phlegm flying from her flaring nostrils. An involuntary roar escapes my throat, not of fear, but of challenge: "I am here. I have my own power, and I am standing my ground. I am not attacking, but I am going my way." I swipe futilely at my sweaty face with my arm, and continue my hopping, snatching progress through the swamp, whipped mercilessly by the wiry bushes. My long summer skirt is enough of a hindrance that I seriously consider ripping it off. I am thinking in terms of steps now, with no chance to look up at the redwings circling my head, protesting my intrusion. Apparently oblivious to the danger and to my un-dignified, absurdly slow progress, my mind chatters on. Is there nowhere wild one can walk in May without invading hotly defended territory? Each step must be carefully plotted to avoid sinking into a couple of feet of water and oozing, soupy mud.

However, at last I am heading away from the nursery, and before long the next few bellows are quieter. Apparently the deer has receded. Now, perversely, I find I am almost sorry. I have not wanted to distress her, but I also do not want to lose touch with her and her riskier world. I have only been seeking sufficient latitude to move beyond the line of her territory. There has been an exhilaration in fencing with her mind and now I regret that I broke that with my yell. I wanted to win her respect, not to cow her.

Soon, the water becomes shallower, and I hop into a field choked with wiry steeple-bush. In this morning of surprises I find I am intensely disap-pointed that the encounter is over. The treacherous question remains in my mind: what if I had walked most slowly and steadily past the doe, avoiding threatening eye contact? Could there have been a middle path, where neither of us gave ground? Alas, I was too civilized to try the experi-ment. But now I am filled with regret. The still lovely day has lost its edge.

To avoid the densest part of the spruce plantation, I have to veer back one last time towards the far side of the doe's thicket. She is still vigilant, and once again she trumpets. And in the ensuing silence, again I miss the electricity, the reality I felt during our confrontation.

Ahead, I find a gateway in the hedgerow that divides the plantation from the orchard field. In the damp mud there I see that this has been the doe's dooryard into the orchard, a favourite winter haunt of deer, where most of the past cold days we saw five or more, wandering like a frieze. Crossing through the gate to the orchard field, I also regret that I have been an intruder, albeit an innocent one, into a world where I plainly have no place. Returned once again to a pastoral, cultivated world, inevitably I have a sense of relief. The difficult walking is over, and survival no longer forces me to pitch my senses high. But there also is sorrow at losing this pitch as well. The drama back in the pine thicket seemed more pungent and powerful by far than my life at home.

Overhead I discover Merak soaring, tentative, gentle, making sure that I see her, skipping one wingbeat when I gladly call her name. As so often, I wish she could share her sightings with me. She surely must have known all along about the doe and her nursery, must have seen the fawn if, as I guessed, it was there. And how many other vital things does she see that I forever will miss? As I trudge back to safety, I feel hopelessly distanced from her world.

Gilean Douglas
(1900 – 1993)

Gilean Douglas was a longtime resident of Cortes Island, British Columbia, and is well known as a writer, journalist and poet. In River for my Sidewalk, *she recounts her life in the Cascade Mountains. Like many other writers in this collection, Douglas rejected the usual conventions of female domestic arrangements and lived alone in a log cabin and survived on her writing and the production of her land. The book was first published under the pseudonym of Grant Madison, since it was assumed that readers would doubt that a woman could survive alone in the wilderness. In this selection Douglas recounts a Christmas spent in the company of the animals around her. The importance of the connection between the human and animal worlds is a repeated theme throughout this anthology and in this selection Douglas echoes the legend that tells of the animals' return to human speech on Christmas Eve, a story which despite its Christian reference, harkens back to Native legends of the connections between the animal and human worlds.*

Merry Christmas To All

from *River for my Sidewalk* (1953)

All day the snow had been coming down; big white flakes that seemed to be falling of their own weight, though they were really as light as the thistledown they covered in my clearing. All day the music of the rivers had been fading, until now it was only a thread of sound — or was it memory? All day the high mountains surrounding my valley had been softly receding. Then they disappeared entirely and opal filled the air where they had been.

It was evening and in the mellow light from my livingroom oil lamp the six-sided space ships came softly, unhurriedly to earth in their tens of trillions. The paths to the rivers, shovelled that morning, were buried again in crystals and beyond them the uncleared trails had become one with drift and rise and hollow. On the fire-scarred mountain I must climb to reach the nearest house four miles away, the snow would be waist deep by now. Too deep for me, loaded with a packsack of gifts and city clothes. This was not ski country and my bearpaw snowshoes had been loaned and lost.

Two days before Christmas and my plans in tatters? Plans to get up at 3 AM and walk over the mountain to connect with a speeder leaving at six for the nearest railroad station. (The branch line had been closed down since the first snowfall in October.) There I was to catch a train for city celebrations in the home of friends. Now I would do none of this at all but spend Christmas, New Year's and probably the rest of the winter snowed in with solitude.

For a few moments I thought regretfully of baths and lights and of warmth which I didn't have to axe into existence; of that glorious promised turkey and the sparkling shop windows. Most of all I thought of good talk and good friends. The door to all this had been slammed shut in my face and as I unpacked the rucksack I would have carried to town I took out a few bright expectations too. But I have always believed that when one door closes another opens. So a door had opened now for me. Where was it and what was behind it?

Having forgotten to reset the time clock in my mind, I woke up promptly at 3 AM. The cabin, flake insulated, was hardly cold though the temperature must have been in its teens. Snowlight and fading moonlight — (the moon had gone down behind the mountains) — gave my bedroom a Regal lily shining. White, blue and pale cerise frost flowers bloomed on every windowpane in this translucency and I grew some of my own by holding a lighted match to "beds" of granular frost. Ferns, fronds and feathers were everywhere, with many Christmassy garlands; and how delighted I was to find the Tannenbaum, the fir tree, over and over again.

But now there was my own Christmas tree to discover, wood to carry, paths to shovel, evergreens to cut for decoration, river ice to break for water, more treats to find for the animals and birds I hoped would come to share them. I went spinning like a top from one inside job to another and then burst out the door into a world of wonder. So still, so white, so gloriously shining; so tall and vast, so utterly filled with snow and solitude. And I, this little I, in the middle of it all. O Life, O Life, I kept saying, this is too much. You have made it all too beautiful. I can hardly bear it.

The snow still fell, but lightly now and I noticed that the flakes were smaller and simpler than the complex forms of yesterday. They had come from the highest clouds, the cirro and the cirrostratus, where lunar and solar halos originate. In fact, the halos are made by light passing through the ice crystals uninterruptedly, from one hexagonal face to another. Light, light, it seemed to run through me like a current that wakened to ecstasy every nerve and vein and sinew. I hugged myself with joy.

The snow stopped, but I didn't. I strung rose hip and western dogwood berries, popcorn I had grown and red huckleberries I had put down in jars. All for the young fir at the forest's edge which would be my living, growing Christmas tree.

Green cookies would go on it and golden doughnuts, scarlet apples, carrot candles, turnip and beet balls. I would share it with the birds, though already their own tree was decorated with suet, seeds in fat, seeds in honey and sunflower seeds alone for the jays and varied thrushes. There was always food on the feeding tray, but this was special.

No browse for the deer, for they were yarded up miles away and the snow between was deep. Porridge with sweet fruit in it for the old coyote, and stew for the wildcat who both came around for a handout, now and then. In case the old and almost toothless cougar arrived he would have both, a washbowl of it near the Christmas tree. The bears would be hibernating surely and the birds wouldn't start coming until dawn. Except for the owls, of course.

Just before dusk I went inside to stir up the fire, but I put on no lights. Munching a sandwich I sat down by the window to watch. The sky had cleared and behind Cougar Mountain the moon was rising. The snow sparkled wherever light touched it and the world outside was a child's dream story before life crumpled the page. But as the moon rose my hopes fell, for two hours had gone by and no guests had come to the feast. Would they come? Would there be a stranger among them to invoke the old Celtic blessing? "Often, often, often goes the Christ in the Stranger's guise."

Then a grey shadow stirred as the coyote sidled slowly out of the cabin's darker shade. He went to the big bowl of porridge placed on the kitchen side of the house, where he usually fed. At that moment I realized that the wildcat bowl was in use too — and was that a lean tawny movement near the forest woodpile? Were those the golden eyes of a great grey owl in the hemlock?

But I forgot them all when I spotted a furry form rolling up the path from the river. A bear, looking like a two-year-old. No, not the same one which had been romping up and down the river all summer, gorging himself on berries. That one had a sharper face. This one hardly seemed to notice his fellow diners, but headed straight for the bird tree — and honey.

I tore into the kitchen, opened a jar of fish and tossed this towards him. The coyote and wildcat jumped away, but came cautiously back again. While bruin was trying to get fish out of the snow I opened more jars. As he was on the seventh, the forest woodpile seemed to lengthen and the old cougar came out into the moonlight. In its kind glow he appeared almost young and invincible. Then he grabbed up the last piece of fish and ambled rather hastily down the garden path. When I looked around my holiday table was empty, except for the ancient one enjoying his porridge-stew and I taking another sandwich out of my pocket.

But for a short while we had all been there, in peace and acceptance; cougar, coyote, wildcat, bear, owl and human. For those moments there had been something between us. A truce? No, more than that; a bond. I became truly part of all life then and for a flash I saw how earth might have been. I was not even startled; only surprised that they had not spoken and the old tales of animals talking on Christmas Eve come alive — again? But perhaps we did "talk" together. The stars glittered, the moon silver-coated the snow, the cougar and I ate. I felt that the others were not too far away, watching.

At least one of them came back, for next morning both trees were wrecks and it didn't look like owl work. But it didn't matter either. I fixed them up again before the birds arrived and Christmas Day feasting began.

That day was a dream of heaven, blue and white and shining. I went through it on wings and wings were all around me; chickadee, wren, kinglet, jay, kingfisher, blackbird, varied thrush, creeper, nuthatch, grosbeak, bunting, redstart, water ouzel and even a willow ptarmigan down from the peaks.

After dark, a pygmy owl hushed in, a saw-whet owl perched on my ridgepole and later still a horned owl came looking for mice that were looking for crumbs. Three of my four-footed friends returned, though not the bear. But he had played the Stranger's part and I was blessed indeed. Now I knew what door had opened and that it would never open for me again in just this way. I looked up at the mountains and the sapphire sky to say thank you, thank you. It seemed so pitifully little for all I had been given.

Place

Catharine Parr Traill
(1802 – 1899)

Catharine Parr Traill is one of Canada's most famous early settlers and nature writers. She was an educated gentlewoman who emigrated to Canada as the wife of an English army officer turned settler. Along with her equally famous sister, Susanna Moodie, Traill documented life in the backwoods of Canada in the 1830s. While her most well-known work is The Backwoods of Canada, *Traill was a prolific author of fiction and non-fiction who also wrote many natural history texts for children as well as adults. In this lesser-known excerpt from* The Backwoods of Canada, *we see the breadth of Traill's botanical knowledge and her desire to find a home in nature by learning her co-habitants. The letter is reminiscent of Gilbert White's* The Natural History and Antiquities of Selborne.

Canadian Wild Flowers

Utility of Botanical Knowledge. — The Fire-Weed. — Sarsaparilla Plants. — Magnificent Water-Lily. — Rice-Beds. — Indian Straw-berry. — Scarlet Columbine. — Ferns. — Grasses.

from *The Backwoods of Canada* (1836)

July 13, 1834

Our winter broke up unusually early this year: by the end of February the ground was quite free from snow, and the weather continued all through March mild and pleasant, though not so warm as the preceding year, and certainly more variable. By the last week in April and the beginning of May, the forest-trees had all burst into leaf, with a brilliancy of green that was exquisitely lovely.

On the 14th, 15th, and 16th of May, the air became suddenly cold, with sharp winds from the north-west, and heavy storms of snow that nipped the young buds and destroyed many of the early-sown vegetable seeds; fortunately for us we were behind hand with ours, which was very well as it happened.

Our woods and clearings are now full of beautiful flowers. You will be able to form some idea of them from the dried specimens that I send you. You will recognize among them many of the cherished pets of our gardens and green-houses, which are here flung carelessly from Nature's lavish hand among our woods and wilds.

How often do I wish you were beside me in my rambles among the woods and clearings: you would be so delighted in searching out the floral treasures of the place.

Deeply do I now regret having so idly neglected your kind offers while at home of instructing me in flower-painting; you often told me the time would come when I should have cause to regret neglecting the golden opportunity before me.

You proved a true prophetess; for I daily lament that I cannot make faithful representations of the flowers of my adopted country, or understand as you would do their botanical arrangement. With some few I have made myself acquainted, but have hardly confidence in my scanty stock of knowledge to venture on scientific descriptions, when I feel conscious that a blunder would be easily detected, and expose me to ridicule and contempt for an assumption of knowledge that I did not possess. The only botanical work I have at my command is Pursh's *North American Flora*, from which I have obtained some information; but must confess it is tiresome blundering out Latin descriptions to one who knows nothing of Latin beyond what she derives through a knowledge of Italian.

I have made out a list of the plants most worthy of attention near us; there are many others in the township that I am a stranger to; some there are with whose names I am unacquainted. I subjoin a slight sketch, not with my pencil but my pen, of those flowers that pleased me particularly, or that possessed any remarkable qualities.

The same plants do not grow on cleared land that formerly occupied the same spot when it was covered with forest trees. A distinct class of vegetation makes its appearance as soon as the fire has passed over the ground.

The same thing may be remarked with regard to the change that takes place among our forests. As one generation falls and decays, new ones of a different character spring up in their places. This is illustrated in the circumstance of the resinous substance called fat-pine being usually found in places where the living pine is least abundant, and where the ground is occupied by oak, ash, beech, maple, and basswood.

The fire-weed, a species of tall thistle of rank and unpleasant scent, is the first plant that appears when the ground has been freed from timbers by fire: if a piece of land lies untilled the first summer after its being chopped, the following spring shows you a smothering crop of this vile weed. The next plant you notice is the sumach, with its downy stalks, and head of deep crimson velvety flowers, forming an upright obtuse bunch at the extremity of the branches; the leaves turn scarlet towards the latter end of the summer. This shrub, though really very ornamental, is regarded as a great pest in old clearings, where the roots run and send up suckers in abundance. The raspberry and wild gooseberry are next seen, and thousands of strawberry plants of different varieties carpet the ground, and mingle with the grasses of the pastures. I have been obliged this spring to root out with remorseless hand hundreds of sarsaparilla plants, and also the celebrated ginseng, which grows abundantly in our woods: it used formerly to be an article of export to China from the States, the root being held in high estimation by the Chinese.

Last week I noticed a succulent plant that made its appearance on a dry sandy path in my garden; it seems to me a variety of the hour-blowing *mesembryanthium*. It has increased to rapidly that it already covers a large space; the branches converging from the centre of the plant, and sending forth shoots from every joint. The leaves are rather small, three-sided and pointed, thick and juicy, yielding a green liquor when bruised like the common sedums. The stalks are thick and round, of a bright red, and trail along the ground; the leaves spring from each joint, and with them a constant succession of yellow starry flowers, that close in an hour or so from the time they first unfold. I shall send you some of the seed of this plant, as I perceived a number of little green pods that looked like the buds, but which, on opening, proved to be the seed-vessels. This plant covers the earth like a thick mat, and, I am told, is rather troublesome where it likes the soil.

I regret that among my dried plants I could not preserve some specimens of our superb water-lilies and irises; but they were too large and too juicy to dry well. As I cannot send you my favourites, I must describe them to you.

The first, then, is a magnificent water-lily, that I have called by way of distinction the "Queen of the Lakes," for she sits a crown upon the waters. This magnificent flower is about the size of a large dahlia; it is double to the heart; every row of petals diminishing by degrees in size, and gradually deepening in tint from the purest white to the brightest lemon colour. The buds are very lovely, and may be seen below the surface of the water, in different stages of forwardness from the closely-folded bud, wrapped in its olive-green calix, to the half-blown flower, ready to emerge from its watery prison, and in all its virgin beauty expand its snowy bosom to the sun and genial air. Nor is the beauty of the flower its sole attraction: when unfolded it gives out a rich perfume not unlike the smell of fresh lemons. The leaves are also worthy of attention: at first they are of a fine dark green, but as the flower decays the leaf changes its hue to a vivid crimson. Where a large bed of these lilies grow closely together, they give quite a sanguine appearance to the waters, that is distinguishable at some distance.

The yellow species of this plant is also very handsome, though it wants the silken texture and delicate colour of the former; I call this the "Water-king." The flower presents a deep golden-coloured cup, the concave petals of which are clouded in the centre with a dark reddish-brown, which forms a striking contrast to the gay anthers; they are very numerous, and turn back from the centre of the flower, falling like fringes of gold one over the other, in successive rows, till they fill up the hollow flower-cup.

The shallows of our lakes abound with a variety of elegant aquatic plants: I know not a more lovely sight than one of these floating gardens. Here you shall behold near the shore a bed of azure fleur-de-lis, from the palest pearl colour varying to the darkest purple. Nearer in shore, in the shallowest water, the rose-coloured *persicaria* sends up its beautiful spikes trailing below the surface; you see the red stalks and smooth dark green leaves veined underneath with rosy red: it is a very charming variety of this beautiful species of plants. Then a bed of my favourite white lilies, all in full bloom, floating on the water, with their double flowers expanding to the sun; near these, and rising in stately pride, a tall plant, with dark green spear-shaped leaves, and thick spike of bright blue flower, is seen. I cannot discover the name of this very grand-looking flower, and I neglected to examine its botanical construction; so can give you no clue by which to discover its name or species.

Our rice-beds are far from being unworthy of admiration; seen from a distance they look like low green islands on the lakes: on passing through one of these rice-beds when the rice is in flower, it has a beautiful appearance with its broad grassy leaves and light waving spikes, garnished with pale yellow green blossoms, delicately shaded with reddish purple, from beneath which fall three elegant straw-coloured anthers, which move with every breath of air or slightest motion of the waters. I gathered several spikes when only just opened, but the tiresome things fell to pieces directly they became dry. Next summer I will make another attempt at preserving them, and it may be with better success.

The low shore of the lake is a complete shrubbery. We have a very pretty St. John's-wort, with handsome yellow flowers. The white and pink spiral frutex also abounds with some exquisite upright honeysuckles, shrubby plants about three feet in height; the blossoms grow in pairs or by fours, and hang beneath the light green leaves; elegant trumpet-shaped flowers of a delicate greenish white, which are succeeded by ruby-coloured berries. On gathering a branch of this plant, you cannot but be struck with the elegant arrangement of the flowers along the under part of the stalks. The two blossoms are connected at the nectary of each in a singular manner. The Americans call this honeysuckle "twinflower." I have seen some of the flowers of this plant pale pink; on the whole it is one of the most ornamental shrubs we have. I transplanted some young bushes into my garden last spring; they promise to live and do well. I know it to be a species of honeysuckle, from the class and order, the shape and colour of the leaves, the stalks, the trumpet-shaped blossom and the fruit, all bearing a resemblance to our honeysuckles in some degree. There is a tall upright bush, bearing large yellow trumpet-shaped flowers, springing from the extremities of the branches; the involucrum forms a boat-shaped cup that encircles the flowers from which they seem to spring, something after the manner of the scarlet trumpet-honeysuckle. The leaves and blossoms of this plant are coarse, and by no means compare to the former.

We have a great variety of curious orchises, some brown and yellow, others pale flesh-coloured, striped with crimson. There is one species grows to the height of two feet, bearing long spikes of pale purple flowers; a white one with most fragrant smell, and a delicate pink one with round head of blossoms, finely fringed like the water-pinks that grow in our marshes; this is a very pretty flower, and grows in the beaver meadows.

Last autumn I observed in the pine-wood near us a very curious plant; it came up with naked brown stems, branching off like some miniature tree; the stalks of this plant were brown, slightly freckled and beset with little knobs. I watched the progress of maturity in this strange plant with some degree of interest, towards the latter end of October; the little knob, which consisted of two angular hard cases, not unlike, when fully opened, to a boat in shape, burst asunder and displayed a pale straw-coloured chaffy substance that resembled fine sawdust: these must have been the anthers, but they bore more resemblance to seeds; this singular flower would have borne examination with a microscope. One peculiarity that I observed was, that on pulling up a plant with its roots, I found the blossoms open under ground, springing up from the lowest part of the flower-stems, and just as far advanced to maturity as those that grew on the upper stalks, excepting that they were somewhat blanched, from being covered up from the air. I can find no description of this plant, nor any person but myself seems to have taken notice of it. The specimen I had on being dried became so brittle that it fell to pieces.

I have promised to collect some of the most singular of our native flowers for one of the Professors of Botany in the Edinburgh University.

The moccasin flower or lady's-slipper (mark the odd coincidence between the common name of the American and English species) is one of our most remarkable flowers; both on account of its beauty and its singularity of structure. Our plains and dry sunny pastures produce several varieties; among these, the *Cypripedium pubescens*, or yellow moccasin, and the *C. Arietinum* are the most beautiful of the species. The colour of the lip of the former is a lively canary yellow, dashed with deep crimson spots. The upper petals consist of two short and two long; in texture and colour resembling the sheath of some of the narcissus tribe; the short ones stand erect, like a pair of ears; the long or lateral pair are three times the length of the former, very narrow, and elegantly twisted, like the spiral horns of the Walachian ram: on raising a thick yellow fleshy sort of lid; in the middle of the flower you perceive the exact face of an Indian hound, perfect in all its parts, — the eyes, nose, and mouth; below this depends an open sack, slightly gathered round at the opening, which gives it a hollow and prominent appearance; the inside of this bag is delicately dashed with deep crimson spots: the stem of the flower is thick towards the upper part, and takes a direct bend; the leaves are large oval, a little pointed and ribbed; the plant scarcely exceeds six inches: the elegant colour and silken texture of the lower lip or bag render this flower very much more beautiful to my taste than the purple and white variety, though the latter is much more striking on account of the size of the flower and leaves, besides the contrast between the white and red, or white and purple colours.

The formation of this species resembles the other, only with this difference, the horns are not twisted, and the face is that of a monkey; even the comical expression of the animal is preserved with such admirable fidelity as to draw a smile from everyone that sees the odd restless-looking visage, with its prominent round black eyes peering forth from under its covering.

These plants belong to class and order *Gynandria diandria*; are described with some little variation by Pursh, who, however, likens the face of the latter to that of a sheep: if a sheep sat for the picture methinks it must have been the most mischievous of the flock.

There is a curious aquatic plant that grows in shallow, stagnant, or slow-flowing waters; it will contain a full wine-glass of water. A poor soldier brought it to me, and told me it resembled a plant he used to see in Egypt, that the soldiers called the "Soldier's drinking-cup;" and "many a good draught of pure water," he said, "I have drank from them."

Another specimen was presented me by a gentleman who knew my predilection for strange plants; he very aptly gave it the name of "Pitcher-plant;" it very probably belongs to the tribe that bear that name.

The flowers that afford the most decided perfumes are our wild roses, which possess a delicious scent: the milkweed, which gives out a smell not unlike the night-blowing stock; the purple monarda, which is fragrance itself from the root to the flower, and even after months' exposure to the wintry atmosphere its dried leaves and seed-vessels are so sweet as to impart perfume to your hands or clothes. All our mints are strong scented: the lily of the valley is remarkable for its fine smell; then there is my queen of the lakes, and her consort, the water-king, with many other flowers I cannot now enumerate. Certain it is that among such a vast assemblage of flowers there are, comparatively, very few that are gifted with fragrant scents. Some of our forest-trees give out a fine perfume. I have often paused in my walks to inhale the fragrance from a cedar swamp on some sunny day while the boughs were still wet with the dew-drops or recently fallen shower.

Nor is the balsam-poplar, or tacamahac, less delightfully fragrant, especially while the gummy buds are just beginning to unfold; this is an elegant growing tree where it has room to expand into boughs. It grows chiefly on the shores of the lakes and in open swamps, but it also forms one of the attractions of our plains, with its silver bark and waving foliage; it emits a resinous clear gum in transparent globules on the bark, and the buds are covered with a highly aromatic gummy fluid.

Our grasses are highly interesting; there are varieties that are wholly new to me, and when dried form the most elegant ornaments to our chimney pieces, and would look very graceful on a lady's head; only fashionists always prefer the artificial to the natural.

One or two species of grass that I have gathered bear a close but of course minute resemblance to the Indian corn, having a top feather and eight-sided spike of little grains disposed at the side-joints. The *sisyrinchium*, or blue-eyed grass, is a pretty little flower of an azure blue, with a golden spot at the base of each petal; the leaves are flat, stiff, and flag-like; this pretty flower grows in tufts on light sandy soils.

I have given you a description of the flowers most worthy of attention; and, though it is very probable some of my descriptions may not be exactly in the technical language of the correct botanist, I have at least described them as they appear.

My dear boy seems already to have a taste for flowers, which I shall encourage as much as possible. It is a study that tends to refine and purify the mind, and can be made, by simple steps, a ladder to heaven, as it were, by teaching a child to look with love and admiration to that bountiful God who created and made flowers so fair to adorn and fructify this earth.

Farewell, my dear sister.

Aleta Karstad
(1951 –)

Aleta Karstad is a well-known painter among whose credits are illustrations for the works of Louise de Kiriline Lawrence and Peri McQuay. She also is the author/illustrator of several natural history works. The Canadian Nature Notebook *captures habitats from across northern North America in text and image.* Moresby Wilderness *(1990) is a facsimile journal of hikes along the coastal trail in the Queen Charlotte Islands. Her forthcoming work,* Fragile Inheritance: A Painter's Ecology of Glaciated North America, *documents the health of habitats across the continent and the way in which people have lived within and altered these places. The selections* "City," "Prairie Wheat Farm" *and* "Tundra" *from the* Canadian Nature Notebook *also emphasize that nature is not just "out there" but part of us and we of it.*

City

from *The Canadian Nature Notebook* (1979)

The city habitat is created and dominated by people. Its main physical features are man-made, and most of its plants are cultivated. The plants and animals which live in cities are a mixture of native species and introductions, deliberate and accidental. Those which are unplanned and unbidden by man are touches of wildness within the city. This chapter is based mainly on Toronto, Ontario, and Quebec City, Quebec.

While people attend to their various concerns inside the big city buildings, birds contest for territories, nest, and raise their young, at home against the outer surfaces of those same buildings. There they find shade in summer, warmth and protection from wind in winter, and a high refuge from the noisy rushing activity of the streets and sidewalks.

Pigeons impress each other by dancing solemnly in circles, this way and that on building ledges, with tails fanned, heads bobbing, and iridescent feathers quivering on inflated necks. A throaty burbling "coo" sounds persistently above the cacophony of mingled traffic noises.

Fat brown House Sparrows swarm in a flock on the pavement, pecking busily at seeds and grit, and picking up popcorn, chips, and crumbs where people drop them. They were introduced from Europe in the 1850s, and since then have evolved adaptations to North American climates, so that House Sparrows from the southern United States are much smaller, and don't use their food as rapidly to keep warm as those in the north.

The melodious twitters and long sliding whistles of a flock of European Starlings liven the still winter air of a residential street, as they feast on the buds of a Silver Maple. Starling plumage looks plain and dark from a distance, but its purple and green iridescence is shot with tiny arrow-heads of cream, and is a delight to be seen at close range.

Buildings provide specialized nest sites for two insect-eating migratory birds. Nesting only inside chimneys, Chimney Swifts have no competition for breeding sites from other species. Nighthawks nest on flat roofs their natural preference being gravelly open places. The sound of them is an integral part of warm summer nights in the city. As traffic noise quiets a little at dusk, the "Bijjjew" calls of high, flycatching Nighthawks and the soft booms they make swooping sharply up from display dives can be heard with the twittering of the circling swifts. Bright lights compensate for the low density of insects in the city, by letting Nighthawks hunt all through the night, instead of only at dusk and dawn.

Backyard bird feeders increase the number of birds that are resident in urban areas in winter. Over time, they may even cause change in the ranges of birds. Food supplied by people in winter has helped the Evening Grosbeak to spread eastward from the Rocky Mountains and the western boreal forest, and the Cardinal and Mockingbird to spread northward into Ontario and Quebec.

Skunks and Racoons are well known in cities as garbage thieves with truculent personalities. Squirrels enjoy a rare position of favour among city wildlife because their boldness and small size appeals to people, and those in parks are tame and well fed. You can spend hours in city parks, watching squirrels forage for buds, seeds, tree flowers, or handouts. They chase each other about trunks and branches, leap wildly between trees from springy branchtips to springy branchtips, and carry bunches of leaves to their winter nests, or drays, high in the trees.

Perhaps the most interesting wild things in the city are those which are unaware of people, and overlooked by people. Small snails with glistening shells inhabit some of the cracks between slabs of sidewalk and against cement walls and foundations, where they feed on algae, low mosses, and the tender shoots of small grasses. Microscopic mites live there too, and tiny gray springtails, brittle brown millipedes, and sowbugs, flat terrestrial crustaceans sometimes called cement bugs. All of these eat very small amounts of dead vegetable matter, and their bodies after death feed each other and fertilize their microhabitat of pavement crack. More mobile and heat-tolerant, small brown ants traverse the broad, sunny stretches of pavement as they forage for anything edible, following the scent trails of those who have found food.

Lawn grass harbours an intricate continuum of comings and goings, easily observed from a prone position with the aid of a hand lens. Leaf hoppers, beetles, tiny moths, spiders, and snails can be seen there by day; and by flashlight, if you are quiet and step carefully, you can watch earthworms feeding and mating in the grass on dewy nights.

A dense, pure mat of lawn grass can only survive where there is plenty of nutrient, moisture, and light. Elsewhere, mowing opens up space, and provides light for the incursion of many small, low, hardy plant species such as Dandelions, chickweed, clovers, and mosses. Everywhere you look about the city there are small undisturbed sites such as the soil around the bases of trees and telephone poles, and along driveways and fences where wild plants grow: plantain, avens, Lychnis, Deptford Pink, Herb Robert, Fleabane, speedwells, buttercups, and several species of mustards. Many of these weeds are wild relatives of showy cultivated flowers, such as Aster, Portulaca, Geranium, Chrysanthemum, and morning glory.

Prairie Wheat Farm

Man has made a different habitat of the prairie by his agricultural practises. This chapter is based mainly on a wheat farm near Brunkild, Manitoba.

Driving west from the spruce forests, Sphagnum bogs, and granite of the shield, or east out of the dusty, rolling cattle country of the western prairies, you find that the land is checkered with brown, green, and gold. The hills are gentle and, in some places, the land is so flat that the telephone poles merge evenly into straight dark ribbons along either side of the highway, which itself grows thinner and nearly disappears before it reaches the far horizon. When the early settlers crossed the plains the tallgrass prairie was an ocean of grass from horizon to horizon, the wind playing like a live thing, dimpling and rolling the wild grass for miles and miles, just as now you see it rippling vast fields of cultivated grasses: wheat, barley, oats, and rye. Now, only the railroad that brought the settlers west preserves the last remnants of tallgrass prairie along its right of way.

In pasture or tallgrass prairie, the insect population is as diverse as the flora, and the many grassland birds nest in the shelter of perennial grassy cover. But in the cultivated monotypic habitat of the grainfield which is harvested every fall and, in winter, lies stark and open to frost and snow, only the insect and fungus pests of grain can live, because there is nothing for any others to eat. Of birds, only the Horned Lark nests in the fields. It raises its brood quickly, feeding them with insects caught along the roads as the crop grows about the nest, and gleaning kernels from the stubble after harvest. When the icy winds of the prairie winter blow over the empty fields the Larks are far away in the southern plains and Mexico. In the more varied habitat along the roads, Western Meadowlarks sing on fence posts, watching over nests well hidden in bowers of roadside grass; young ground squirrels pop in and out of burrows, flicking tails, and wrestling and squealing; Killdeers incubate clutches of four speckled eggs on the flat, gravelly road shoulders; but only the Horned Larks, ground-nesting seed eaters, are adapted for life in a field of grain.

Wherever man establishes himself on the open prairie he plants windbreaks — narrow groves of trees along fencerows and all around his house and buildings, or just a single line of Cottonwoods, Manitoba Maples, or willows if the ground is wet — across the path of the prevailing west wind. Thus he creates for himself a comfortable microclimate, shelter from the harshness of the sun and the relentless force of great masses of air, blowing unchecked from high pressure areas to low pressure areas across the flat land. Storms can come quickly, looming purple-gray on the horizon, heavy clouds pushing toward you; you can smell the nearness of rain. The air grows alarmingly still and dark, and the leaves hang waiting. Robins, kingbirds, doves, orioles, Starlings, and Grackles fly to their nests to protect eggs and young as the first tentative drops spit from the sky. You can see the wind rushing like a herd of invisible bison, bending young wheat to the ground. When it reaches the windbreak, the trees seem to leap out of their stillness, swaying, tossing their branches, leaves all turning silver backsides. The lashing boughs of aspen and Cottonwood hiss and scintillate as their leaves flutter and rattle. Rain streams down in sheets and water pours from the gutters of the roofs. The soil has turned from gray to black and puddles form where a few moments ago it was cracked and dry.

Sometimes, instead of lifegiving rain, the storm brings hail, hurling tons of hard ice to the earth, breaking stems, cutting off ripening heads of grain, chopping wheat into acres of worthless grass clippings. Imagine the sight of green crops turned into ploughed fields by the force of hail! Wet years occur, when low areas flood and must be reseeded, or the soil remains too soft and wet to bear planting machinery. Dry years come too, when soil is blown for miles, filling in ditches and settling out of the air inside houses and barns. Seed is scattered, exposed on the roads, and drifted into ditches with the dust.

But now it is raining. The face of the storm has passed and steady drops fall from a dull, white sky. Robins and Brewer's Blackbirds search for worms on the fresh, bright grass of the lawn, and doves mince across the gravel by the barn. Kingbirds flash from tree to tree, calling and checking their territories for intruders, and swoop suddenly from leafy perches after passing flies and flying beetles. Insects are on the move, out of hastily taken shelter, and birds are hunting them, eager to find and eat those that were knocked down and wet by the rain. Barn Swallows are fly-catching, lacing the space above the barnyard in an aerial ballet, their rusty breasts glowing within silhouettes of narrow wings and forked tails.

Many bird species make use of the planted windbreaks of the prairie farms, returning every year to the trees that they know to nest and raise their young. Black and orange orioles meticulously weave swinging nests high in the trees. Several pairs of Robins construct twiggy nests close to the trunks of Apple and Box Elder, as do kingbirds. They arrive from the south later than the Robins, and sometimes a Robin may find its eggs on the ground and its nest occupied by a pair of kingbirds, even more aggressive than themselves, and willing to fight anything with wing, beak, and claw.

The yodelling coo of Mourning Doves sounds soft in the evening from fir boughs and barn lofts. These subtly iridescent dawn-beige birds build very flimsy nests. The best way to view the eggs is from beneath, through spaces in the nest. Often an egg or two will roll out, when the dove flushes in a whirr at someone's approach. Doves cannot defend their nests, so, if a nest is slight, perhaps it is less noticeable to egg predators. Doves make pigeon's milk in their crops, which enriches regurgitated food with protein, and makes it possible to raise three or four broods a year.

While I was in a tangled willow windbreak beside a dugout pond, a pair of Robins was very disturbed, hopping about from branch to branch above me. They squeaked sharply and constantly, "Peerp, peerp, peerp, peerp, peerp, peerp, peerp," with head feathers raised, rusty breasts fluffed, and eyes blinking in indignation. Then I found the nest, only a meter above the ground, where a nearly fledged young Robin hunched, still, watching me. The racket of its parents' scolding made me feel uneasy. A chalky-breasted Eastern Kingbird made his hostile appearance, with tiny scarlet crest lifted. Drawn by the commotion, a male Redwinged Blackbird, trilling fiercely, and a vivid black and orange Baltimore Oriole, were ready to mob. Predator discouragement is a community effort. Chastened, I left, flushing another young Robin into clumsy flight from a nearby branch.

House sparrows appreciate farm buildings, clustering around spoiled grain like flies, and nesting under eaves and behind gutter pipes. In the spring, House Wrens pop in and out of any hole that is just the right size, searching for nesting places, sometimes getting trapped in the house. Barn swallows cheep and chatter as they build sturdy nests of mud balls, with bits of string and feathers for extra strength, on rafters and under ledges, and especially inside, if there is always a way in and out. They often renovate the same nest year after year, and become accustomed to the presence and noise of people and machinery, coming and going about the tasks of the wheat farm.

On the open prairie, the scattered groups of planted trees are oases for migrating birds in spring and fall. Then you may see Red-eyed Vireos, Swainson's Thrushes, Yellow Warblers, Redstarts, and Song Sparrows from the aspen parkland; Juncos, White-throated sparrows, Red-breasted Nuthatches, and Myrtle Warblers from the boreal forest; and Black-poll Warblers, and White-crowned and Harris sparrows from the edge of the tundra.

The farm is shared by much more than birds. A family of skunks may have lived for several generations under an old granary, and earned the respect of many farm dogs. The white stripes of the skunks' long soft coats gleam in the darkness as they nose their nocturnal way across the dewy lawn, hunting earthworms and, after spring rains, Tiger Salamanders, and snuffling under old logs and boards in the windbreak for beetles and grubs. The mask-faced Racoon, who sleeps in the great hollow trunk of the oldest willow, catches frogs in the grass, feels for crayfish at the muddy edge of the dugout, and raids the garden by night for ripe sweet corn. The ever-present voles live their mouse-lives in the grassy margins of the windbreaks, and in fallow fields. They are prey for Red-tailed Hawks and Harriers in summer, and Rough-legged Hawks and Snowy Owls in winter. Large-eyed Deer Mice, with immaculately white feet and bellies, skitter secretly through their trails and tunnels, more secure in the shelter of trees or buildings. A shy Red Fox, whose den is somewhere out of sight where the ground is well drained, hunts mice and ground squirrels in the morning and evening.

Some farms have rectangular dugouts, made for domestic water supply, or for livestock. You will find the banks pelted with dark green sedge, starred with yellow buttercups, lined with tall cattails, and leaping with Leopard Frogs. Burrowing crayfish may lurk in its muddy bottom, and each year it is a nursery for Mallards or teal.

Tundra

The tundra has a great variety of plant communities that grow on permanently frozen ground between the boreal forest and the limit of plant growth. In North America it covers all of the Arctic Archipelago and vast areas of the mainland in Labrador, northwest of Hudson's Bay, and around Alaska to the Aleutian Islands. This chapter is based on observations made on the Cumberland Peninsula of Baffin Island; and in Churchill, Manitoba.

Lying on a flat place of dry tundra or sitting against a hummock for a near ground level view across the dry tundra, you will find that only rocks rise above the narrow seed heads of hardy summer grasses. The strong, twisted gray trunk by your side does not aspire to height and, if you can forget the scale of the world where trees are tall, you will respect this willow as an old and great tree, telling the tundra story of more than a hundred springs.

You are sitting on trees — willows that are not even the shape of bushes but part of the herb mat itself. With shiny, crinkly, oval leaves and large pink catkins, they push their way through moss and lichens to share the sunlight during long summer days. The willows and heaths here grow slowly, because warmth, water, and nutrients are of limited supply. The low, thickly tangled plant community crowds its branches, twigs, and evergreen leaves into a dense mat, insulating itself from the freezing temperatures which are frequent during the short summer. Here there is little rain. Most of the precipitation falls in winter as snow and, in summer, plants which do not have access to a continuing supply of snow meltwater live in desert conditions.

In moist depressions and in the shelter of cliffs, bluffs, and boulders, shrubby birches and gnarled bushes of willow spread their branches in low domed shapes. Their profiles trace the height and placement of the snowdrifts that protected them from extreme winter cold and wind. With them, in this ideal microhabitat, grow Crowberry, the purple-flowered evergreen *Phyllodoce*, Labrador tea, low, tangled Cranberry and Bilberry mat, and patches of reindeer moss lichen. All are bedded in a fine tangled layer of roots and stems, dead and alive, and packed all through with mosses.

Where snow is swept from the rocks by wind, or where it melts early on hilltops and high, flat ground, the terrain is barren except for a few lichens, notably the yellow *Cetraria nivalis*. In the shelter of boulders there, the early, pink-flowered *Saxifraga oppositofolia* grows alone in sparse, sprawling mats on sand and gravel. On dry slopes where the snow melts early, the herb mat is very low and thin. Yellow-flowered *Dryas integrifolia* is well adapted for drought with tough, shiny little evergreen leaves, thickly massed together in isolated patches.

As the edges of deep snowdrifts melt in spring and summer, they expose the glossy dark green foliage of *Cassiope tetragona*, a white-flowered bell heather, which needs the moisture of the melting snow. Later melting reveals small, light green pairs of round Herb Willow leaves, with wet-loving saxifrages, fast-growing Dwarf Buttercups, sorrel, dandelions, and a few small grasses. Briefly uncovered by the last of the drifts, and always quite wet, are the dark green spikes of the sedge *Luzula*.

Where the snow melts the latest, some very short mosses and a film of algae may cover the otherwise bare wet soil. So, even after the last of the snow has gone in late summer, the patterns of the plants tell where it has been, and for how long.

Above the unyielding frozen ground called permafrost, the soil softens in spring and flows slightly down slopes, settling in a pattern of gentle, regular ribs and grooves. Often the slightly moister grooves can by distinguished from the ridges by a difference in the tone and texture of plant life. *Cassiope* darkens the grooves there, and also in the moist cracks of *tundra polygons*, which are kept open by water seepage and autumn freezing. In wet meadows, "tussocks" of ground are forced up by the expanding of freezing water in the surface of the meadow. These elevations support mosses, lichens, and many plants of the dry heath. Around and between the tussocks grow the wet-tolerant mosses, the fluffy flowered sedge called cotton grass, and the short sedge *Luzula*.

In spring, the tundra is alive with birds that migrate from the south to breed. Plovers, godwits, phalaropes, jaegers, Horned Larks, Redpolls, Lapland Longspurs, Snow Buntings, and Savannah, Tree, and Harris sparrows are only a few of the many birds which come from the south for the short tundra summers. The birds which live in the tundra year-round are few. These are Rock and Willow ptarmigans, eaters of twigs, buds, and seeds, the scavenging Raven, and two birds of prey, the Snowy Owl and the Gyrfalcon.

In the lee of a large boulder, flatly decorated by gracefully twined willow branches, a ptarmigan has left a handful of light, dry, curved droppings. Near the rock you may also find owl pellets, chunks of silvery gray matted hair, feathers, and small whole lemming bones, regurgitated by Snowy Owls as they sat there watching the tundra. The droppings of Arctic Foxes contain bones as well, but crushed by the foxes' teeth, and not as easy to identify. Caribou bones and antlers, and even the ribs and vertebrae of sea mammals dragged by Wolves or foxes to seaside tundra, are spotted easily as they lie where meals were finished long ago. Animal remains decompose slowly in this cold, dry habitat, and are visible, stark and white, for years while the herb mat slowly closes over them.

Mary Majka
(1927 –)

Daughter of a Czechoslovakian countess and a Polish school principal, Mary Majka came early to her love for nature when as a child she hiked with her father on the Russian border. She also came early to her determination to do something to save nature when as an eight-year-old she organized her schoolmates into the Society for the Protection of our Garden. Separated from her mother after her father's death, Majka spent World War II working on a farm in the Austrian Alps. She married her husband Mike while they were doing medical training in Austria. They emigrated to Canada in 1961. Since that time she has led many environmental campaigns to protect wildlife and save endangered habitats. She lives in the isolated community of Marys' Point on the Bay of Fundy and acts as the warden and protector of the area which is one of the most important locations on the pathways of migrating shorebirds. In **Fundy National Park** *she combines natural and human history with an introduction to the park and the importance it plays in her own life.*

Waters Slow, Waters Swift

from *Fundy National Park* (1977)

Let's take a trip to a pond. The best time is the early morning when the mist is rising. Cautiously approaching we can listen for and maybe even spot some birds. Pond edges are favourite nesting and feeding places for birds. Busy swallows dart to and fro catching insects "on the wing." Their nests are not far removed.

Should our pond be McLaren Pond, in the park, the nesting sites would be the eaves of the surrounding buildings. In the tall shrubs and trees that lean over the calm waters other birds sing and flit about. Warblers such as the yellow throat and redstart like to nest near the water; we may glimpse the nest of a yellow warbler through the leaves. Sometimes, a duck or even a bittern might settle down on the floating island for a while.

The sun quickly burns off the mists and dries the water lily leaves. This is the time for dragonflies and the smaller damselflies that emerged from their nymphal skins during the night to dry their wings and take off on a busy round of visits in search of a mate.

Who else do we find at the pond? Of course, the frogs. A pond would not be a pond without them and McLaren is not an exception. The green frog's deep voice can be heard at night and also in early misty mornings. So let's look where the frogs are, to see what they are up to.

The babies, the tadpoles, are below the surface while their parents sit motionless on the shore or on lily pads waiting for passing insects. Since McLaren Pond is the deepest body of water in the park we wouldn't really like to jump in but we can peek into the water at the shallower edges or dip a net. The amazing variety and number of swimming, crawling, and jumping creatures will surprise us. One of the busiest and most numerous is the water boatman. At close range, we can see where it got its name.

Tiny oars propel it quickly through the miniature underwater jungle. It is closely followed by another bug which has elected to swim on its back. Its name, of course, is "back swimmer." It preys on anything smaller than itself.

This is not so with the nymph of the beautiful dragonfly which, ferocious and ugly looking, prowls around in search of creatures even bigger than itself and can tackle even a fish or small frog. It does this with ease since its lower jaws are flexible.

Larvae of various insects, including the pesky mosquito, like to live in ponds and still waters. Two large swimmers encountered in the pond are the giant water bug and the water beetle. Snails and tiny fresh water clams can be found on the bottom.

There are also plants that prefer warm and calm waters — the lily, or spatterdock, the arrowhead, the pickerel weed, and at the edges of the pond, the bullrush and cattail. These are the plants that keep their heads high and dry; others live submerged. One of these is a relative of the bladderwort we find in the bogs. It is a strange plant that can catch and digest the tiny organisms of the pond. Little bladders attached to its leaves act as traps.

Streams and Rivers

All of the streams and rivers in Fundy National Park eventually end up in the Bay of Fundy. They start in the higher parts of Albert County and many of them drain the lakes of the park. Near their beginning they are slow, sluggish streams but after a short distance they tumble down forming waterfalls and pools only to slow down at the end of their journey to the bay.

Water is always an attraction for plants and animals. Along the streams, ferns and orchids, violets, touch-me-nots, and all the plants that prefer moist places grow profusely. The bird life along the stream is also more interesting and varied. Animals come to drink and browse on the lush vegetation or to look for food on the shores of the brook. Some fish prefer the cool running streams, especially the salmon which sometimes enter even small brooks to spawn. The other common fish of the streams is the speckled trout; also the rainbow trout which is an introduced species. The cool swift waters harbour insect larvae and nymphs which require more oxygen than their counterparts in ponds. Caddis fly larvae are not always easy to find since they surround themselves with small pebbles and other debris. Black fly larvae live on rocks along with May-fly larvae. Racoons look for fresh water mussels. Mink and otter hunt near the shores of streams and rivers and dive for fish and frogs. In much of New Brunswick the wood turtle is common but none have been found in the park. For moose and deer ponds and rivers are important as both water sources and feeding areas. Moose especially like water plants and find cooling and soothing relief from mosquito and black fly bites.

All the other larger bodies of water in the park are lakes. Although of various sizes, they have similar characteristics. Surrounded by forest, they are fed by small brooks and springs. Some are used for recreation such as swimming, boating, fishing and picnicking. Others are more remote and wild and are used mostly by wildlife. Most of the lakes have been stocked with trout to compensate for the numbers being fished out each year by visitors. Life at the edges of a lake differ little from the life we described at the edge of McLaren Pond. Remote lakes attract water birds and so, black ducks, ring-necked ducks and bitterns build their nests on the edges. Otter, muskrat and beaver are also lake dwellers.

Some of Fundy's lakes have an interesting inhabitant, the newt. That small salamander lives a "triple life." The eggs hatch into slender greenish tadpoles which soon develop legs and lungs and crawl out onto land where their colour changes to bright rusty red. They are then called red efts. After growing on land for a year they return to the water as mature individuals ready to mate. They acquire beautiful light green sides spotted with red and brilliant yellow bellies. Their tail develops a fin well-suited for swimming. They remain in the water for the rest of their lives.

Where the Caribou Roamed

The upper part of the park, a rather flat plateau, has very poor drainage. The water flow from depressions was often blocked by the silt and mud dumped by the glaciers. Sphagnum moss, growing in the small swampy lakes, gradually filled them with peat on which other plants could grow.

That is how bogs are formed. The most accessible and certainly best known bog in the park is the Caribou Plain. Caribou actually lived on this bog. The last of those magnificent animals here was hunted and shot at the turn of the century. Quite a few Albert County inhabitants remember the caribou or have heard about it from their parents. It is believed that this animal became extinct in this area not only because of excessive hunting but also because of scarcity of lichens on which they feed. Lichens grow profusely on mature trees and the lumber industry gradually diminished the number of old trees in the area. Today, the Caribou Plain could be termed an old bog. Very, very gradually trees are invading its borders and eventually, in a few thousand years. it will be covered with forest. This slow pace can be realized when one examines the invading trees. Their stunted little trunks, when cut, reveal them to be fifty to a hundred years old.

The smaller plants of a bog are equally exciting. The pitcherplant awakes everyone's curiosity. Its leaves and flower do not resemble any other plant nor does its habit of feeding on insects. The name "pitcherplant" comes from the pitcher-shaped leaf. Water collects inside the "pitcher" and insects, enticed by the red colour of the veins, crawl inside and drown. The upper part of the inside of the leaf is lined with fine hairs, all pointing downwards, to prevent insects from crawling out. The plant absorbs minerals from the rotting, drowned insects, thus supplementing its poor diet derived from the sphagnum floor. An interesting phenomenon can be seen inside the leaf of the pitcher plant. Beside the drowned bodies of insects, one can find the small white aquatic larvae of a fly which lays its eggs only in the pitcherplant leaves. Another carnivorous plant found here is the sundew. Much smaller and more delicate, it traps its prey on the sticky droplets of the hairy leaves.

The bladderwort is another curious plant found in bogs. Its yellow snapdragon-like flowers protrude through the sphagnum. The very tiny leaves are hidden among the moss.

At Caribou Plain, as in many other bogs, there is a small lake. At the lakeshore, cottongrass with its white plume adds to the colour and beauty of the bog. In the upper areas a tiny raspberry, baked-apple-berry, blossoms with a single flower to produce a delectable fruit which surprisingly enough tastes like baked apple. In areas of extensive bogs, such as northeastern New Brunswick and Newfoundland, this berry is picked in great quantities and is a favourite of local people. Labrador tea is another edible plant, an old standby of wood travellers and trappers. Ferns that prefer wet habitats and acid soils also border the bogs. One of them, very common in the Caribou Plain area, can be easily recognized by its separate flowering stalk which bears spores of golden cinnamon colour, hence the name Cinnamon fern.

The characteristics of bogs found in the park vary, depending very much on their age. The older ones are covered with cranberries, crowberries, Labrador tea, sheep laurel and rhodora, the younger ones with sphagnum moss and various lichens. The red-backed mouse is one of the few bog mammals.

The bog is exciting not only because it has unusual plants and animals but also because its flora and fauna represent a community that is typical of areas found much further north in Labrador and northern Quebec. This is because of the cool temperature of the mossy ground during summer.

Salt Marsh and the Bog

The salt marsh is a very different world from the freshwater marsh. Different plants, animals and insects inhabit each. There are no appreciable freshwater marshes in Fundy National Park. There is only a small salt water marsh at the mouth of the Alma River just at the entrance of the park. Small as it is, it is an interesting and exciting place to visit.

Many fish spawn in the shallow recesses of this marsh. Lush green algae cover the many ponds where ducks, great blue herons and yellowlegs feed. Geese sometimes rest there during migration and the cousin of the beaver, the muskrat, builds his haystack home in the grassy expanses along its meandering creeks.

The Beaver

When the white man first arrived on this continent, streams and lakes swarmed with beaver. Not only was the beaver's skill in building dams and lodges admired, but his fur became the most valuable commodity. Indians traded beaver pelts for guns and blankets. "Castoreum," the secretion of a beaver's gland, was believed to be a cure for all ills. It strengthened man and gave him good sight. It cured pleurisy and apoplexy, sciatica and deafness. Powdered beaver teeth were supposed to have special healing powers and the tail was a favourite delicacy. Luckily for the beaver, European fashions changed and so the export of pelts diminished. But for a very long time such was the demand for beaver skins that today historians credit the beaver with being responsible to a large degree for the opening up of this continent. French voyageurs and English explorers bartered with the Indians, blazing trails for the settlers who followed.

"Busy as a beaver" is an understatement. An architect and a mason, woodcutter and a hauler, he is capable of building a dam that will hold thousands of cubic feet of water. He is renowned for his work in water conservation. Sometimes his "services" are used where there are water storage problems.

Beavers do not hibernate and so with the approach of winter they gather a good supply of twigs and branches and store them underneath the water. "The bigger the pile, the longer the winter" — as many good woodsmen will tell you.

My Friend the Beaver

At dawn when I come to the edge of the water, I hope to see him. The mist over the river valley has just begun to move slowly towards the sea. Like a phantom stream it silently folds, descends and rises, enfolding trees, leaves and grasses with soft moisture which will later turn to diamonds of dew. For the moment everything is calm … Suddenly I see my friend gliding out of the mists and steering toward our usual meeting place. Alert and carefully watching the shores, he spots me! In a playful greeting he slaps his tail and disappears into the milky water, to emerge just a few feet from me. I sit very still and hold his favourite cattail root in my hand — waiting.

My heart beats rapidly — will he climb up the bank and approach me, or just swim around me in circles and wait until I throw my offering into the water? But his little eyes are trusting and seem to smile. Ripples of water have reached me now and splash quietly against the grassy shore all strewn with the debris of my friend's work — pieces of branches and twigs, chewed and cut up by his skilful teeth.

He lands on a gravelly spot and walks hesitantly towards me. I stretch my arm as far as I can without moving my body. He stops and sits up, propping himself with his flat tail, holding his forepaws in front of his powerful chest. He sits and looks at me for what seems an eternity. Water still splashes over the bank. It is so still, so wonderfully cool and almost eerie in that misty valley. Right now dream and reality can meet and mingle freely.

I look at my friend and talk to him without words. I am telling him that for many hours every morning of this summer I came and sat here. That I have dug and stored great quantities of cattail roots — just for him, so they can last for a long time — maybe for his winter? That I want to be his friend and know more about him.

He listens intently, showing his yellow teeth and twitching his long whiskers. Suddenly he simply trods towards my outstretched hand. I feel his wet paws. For a second they clasp my fingers, as in greeting — and then he is gone for another day!

I walk slowly up from the river and watch the mists lift — like a rosy veil of the rising sun. Birds are starting to assemble their orchestra, trying out parts of today's symphony. Somewhere below, on the edge of his lodge, my friend the beaver has finished munching on his chunk of cattail and is turning in for a day's rest, after a busy night.

Merilyn Simonds Mohr
(1949 –)

Merilyn Simonds Mohr was born in Winnipeg, Manitoba, spent her childhood in Brazil, reared her own children in northern Ontario, and currently lives in Kingston, Ontario. A freelance writer for the past fifteen years, her articles have appeared in Harrowsmith, Equinox *and* Saturday Night *magazines. For several years she was contributing editor for* Harrowsmith, *specializing in environmental issues. In 1989 she won the Greg Clark Award for outdoor writing and in 1990 she won a Science Writers of Canada award. She has published ten books, most recently* The Convict Lover *(1996). This essay was first published in* Harrowsmith *magazine under the title "Promises of Spring." It will be the title story of a collection of memoirs she is working on at present.*

Stubborn Particulars of Place
(1991)

At the beginning of the last century, my great-great-grandmother, Mary Cornfoot, left her home in Aberdeen, Scotland, sailed to Canada and walked north with her grown children from the end of the rail line in Orillia, Ontario, to a scrap of land she had purchased, sight unseen, near what is now the town of Gravenhurst. If her husband came with her, there is no record of him. Nor do I know what she thought when she saw the foreboding rocks and trees that greeted her. What I do know is that they felled the maples and pines, cleared the land, made the landscape their own. For all their hard work, it remained, after all, a stone farm, yielding crop after crop of granite and little else. Only the stone piles grew. They stayed on, for a while. There are streets in Gravenhurst named for her grandson: George Street, Elder Street. The log house, added to and shored up by someone else's forebears, and Mary's gravestone — an obelisk of grey granite — are still there, but the family eventually dispersed, and by the time I was born our connection with that part of the province was largely mythological.

So when I moved to North Bay with my husband in 1977, my immediate affection for the north caught me unawares. I had lived all my life in the south, in the flamboyant, overbearing tropics of Brazil and the fertile farmland of southwestern Ontario. By comparison, the spare boreal forest and recalcitrant rock seemed a restrained and exacting landscape indeed. Our first spring on Stonehill Acres, fifty acres of second-growth conifers interrupted here and there by shoulders of rock that shrugged out of the ground, I often thought of Mary. Was she, like me, drawn by its indifference?

Every day, I walked in the bush, ostensibly to pull the skeletons of decomposing wrecks to the road so they could be carted off to the dump

— every northern property, it seems, has a few derelict cars buried on its back forty. I returned with a steering wheel one day, a door the next, then a fender, and once, a windshield, intact, that I positioned in front of hay bales, facing south, to give the bunching onions an early start.

As I parted the undergrowth to reveal yet another chassis and dragged hood after hood by its corroded ornament to the road, I became familiar with more than the anatomy of automobiles. Inside the rotted hulk of a 1940s Dodge, coils of filigreed green poked through the back seat. Near the edge of the clearing where our house stood, a twining plant with maple-like leaves and spiny gourds embroidered a bumper. The forest floor was cushioned with stiff little clutches of dark, glossy leaves; the red berries, when I crushed them between my fingers, smelled faintly of mint. There were loftier plants, too, with slender, May-green leaves waving over shorter stalks of berries. Soon, I was carrying Peterson in my parka pocket, and learning from him the names of these plants that were my new neighbours: the fiddleheads and wild cucumbers, the wintergreens and sarsaparilla.

Eventually, there came an end to the scraps of rusted metal that I could haul to the road, but the walks continued. I no longer needed an alibi. Unabashedly, I commiserated with the bladder campion on its name, gave the ironwood tree a friendly tap, congratulated the black cherry on the profusion of its blooms and did what I could to relieve the hazelnut bushes and pin cherry trees of the shrouds spun by voracious caterpillars. In the winter, when the snow was thigh deep, I made my rounds on snowshoes and skis, translating the hieroglyphics of hoofprint and spoor, occasionally sighting the moose or wolf that had made them. Birdsong remained, for the most part, an undifferentiated concerto, but I did learn to recognize by sight the jays and owls and four kinds of grosbeak that lived in our woods, the buntings and warblers I glimpsed as they passed through to warmer wintering grounds. I never felt the urge to follow. Every year, the landscape was becoming more mine; every year, more distinctly itself.

At one end of the property, just west of the clearing, was a massive upheaval of granite that rose abruptly from a stream. Early one June, I crossed the water, swollen by spring run-off, on a bridge made of two poles, then climbed The Big Rock, levering myself up the mossy slope by crooking my arms around the saplings that seemed to poke straight out of barren stone. The top of the granite outcropping was almost perfectly flat, the edges fringed with alders and balsam fir, weed trees that somehow got a foothold in the first folds of the uplifted rock. On the north edge, in an indentation so shallow that it might have been made by the heel of my palm, a solitary pink lady's slipper grew in a patch of moss. Until now there had been only the dangling chartreuse bells of the Solomon's Seal and the pale umbrels of wild leek. The lady's slipper was the first flower of colour. It held its head high in the forest, drooping its leaves so that its sensuous lower lip would be more prominently displayed.

Back at the house, I pulled from the kitchen shelf a turn-of-the-century household guide given to me by my great-aunt Mabel. Sure enough, *Mother's Remedies* listed Lady's Slipper in the "Herb Department," right after Juniper and before Life Root. The flower was a Valerian, a member of the orchid family that grows, uncharacteristically, in cool climates. "Taken for delirium," the book said.

I remembered orchids from my youth, clusters of pale yellow flowers staring down at me from between the lianas in the Bosque, a bit of preserved jungle that passed for a park in the Brazilian city where I grew up. Worm-like roots clutched at the tree trunk; splayed, crimson tongues thrust from between the puckered white lips of the waxy blooms. Their petals splattered with speckles the colour of dried blood. Their little animal faces terrified me. Could this elegant bloom, rising from the granite floor, really be a distant relative?

Lady's Slipper. It was not a name I would have chosen for it. I looked it up in *The Private Lives of Orchids*, hoping for a more appropriate nickname. No such luck. Lady's Slippers grow in temperate climates around the world and though the connotation shifts from practical to religious to fanciful, cultures are apparently unanimous in their choice of central image: in German, *Frauenschuh*, woman's shoe; in Russian, *Mariin Bashnachock*, Mary's Slipper; in French, *Sabot de Vénus* or *Sabot de la vierge*, Venus' shoe or shoe of the virgin; in Ojibway, *Neemidi moccasin*, Dancing Slipper. To the settlers of this country, they were moccasin flowers, squirrel shoes. Even the Greek name of the genus — *Cypripedium* — means Aphrodite's little shoe. Stubbornly, I held to my contention that there was little that was pediform in the Lady Slipper's translucent pink, swollen sac. Lady's Purse, perhaps, or Pouting Plant or Pregnant Polly. Despite the fact that "orchid" derives from the Greek word for testicle — some orchids have a pair of tuberous roots that look remarkably like male genitalia — there was something undeniably female about this particular flower.

Every spring for ten years, May was punctuated with trips to the rock to look for signs of her arrival. I fussed over that patch of moss, straining for a glimpse of a pale green sprout, hardly able to keep myself from poking in the soil to see if she was stirring. The anticipation made me delirious. It was like waiting for a favourite aunt to appear for her annual visit: you haven't heard from her all year, you don't know if she's still alive, you aren't sure if you've come to the train station on the right day, or even if this is the right station. All the indentations in the rock began to look familiar; other patches of moss tried to trick me with sprouts of painted trillium and Canada mayflower. It had been a year, I thought in despair when she still had not appeared by the end of May, and a lot can happen in a year.

But the lady's slipper never failed me. One day late in the second spring, beside the dry, broken twig that I recognized as last year's flower stalk, a spike pushed through the ground, its tightly furled leaves gradually unfolding to reveal, inside the second, innermost leaf, a stem. Well, not a stem really, because the Latin name for this species — *acaule* — means stemless. It was a flower stalk that grew directly from the base of the plant, between the two leaves. And on top of this tall stalk eventually uncurled the most exquisite flower I have ever known.

It was always worth the wait. Four wisps of brownish tissue — two sepals and two petals, virtually indistinguishable and already parchment crisp — spread their arms like a cross. From the centre drooped a pendulous pink sac formed by two opposing petals folding themselves together, like the sleeves of a silk kimono. When, a few days after the bloom first emerged, I took a break from gathering wild strawberries in the field beside the house, I noticed a bee disappear inside the bulging lower lip of the lady's slipper. Could this beauty be carnivorous? I got down on my hands and knees. At the bottom of the sac, I saw a cleft in the petals. The pink flesh was so translucent that I could see the shadow of the bee buzzing about inside. I was reminded of something I once read — that prisons have "pink rooms" where violent offenders are taken to calm themselves — and I wondered if the bee was relaxing in its rosy room. Within a few seconds, the insect emerged from a small hole on the right side of the top of the sac. What had it been doing in there?

I could not bring myself to pick the flower to probe the intimacies of its structure. Others had. The vibrant pink colour and sweet fragrance of the lady's slipper, it seemed, attracted bees to enter the slit in the front of the sac. But it was a one-way door: the petals folded inward. At the top of the pink lip were two exits; inside they were light-coloured and flagged with nectar-coated hairs to attract the bee, who had probably tippled a little before it crawled out. As the bee exited, it brushed past a little round green knob — the male parts of the lady's slipper — that left pollen stuck to its back. On the front of the flower, between the two exits, was a bright green pad that the bee also brushed against — the female part of the flower. As it moved from lady's slipper to lady's slipper, the bee was collecting and depositing pollen. For its trouble, it got a few sips of nectar in the pinkest of salons. Not a bad deal.

Over the next few years, most of the plants and birds I came to know I associated with a certain season. Spring began with the return of the tree sparrows with their rusty caps and little stickpin breasts. Tiny blue violets bloomed in the ditch and, for a brief time, the woods at the edge of the field were carpeted with trilliums, only rarely white, more often their ominous blood-red relatives, the Death Flower, and occasionally, petals edged in navy blue and streaked with deep purple. Blue flags bloomed, whether planted by some previous owner or wild, I could not tell. As the days warmed, the wild calla down by the stream would unfold its white spathe to reveal a stiff little spadix covered with tiny yellow flowers. And in the woods, from the centre of a whorl of bright green leaves the brilliant white starflower would emerge. By midsummer, the clearing was daubed with black-eyed Susans, daisies, Devil's paintbrush and purple vetch, the ditches thick with bouncing Bet, St. John's wort and milkweed. Chokecherries dripped from the hedgerows. Then, the Indian hemp bloomed with its waxy pink bells and the pokeberries began to darken. Before long, the vireos were gorging themselves on bunchberries and it was time to pick the pearly everlastings.

But through it all there was the lady's slipper, a constant warp thread in my developing fabric of colours and textures and sounds. It outlasted the summer. When it first bloomed in early June, the flower sepals and petals were guarded over by one slender green leafy bract. As the flower faded, the shaft between the bract and the sepals began to grow. By August, the bloom had shrivelled to a brownish-pink rag and the fruit swelled, lifting itself up until the inch-long seed casing poked brazenly into the wind. Sometime late in the summer, the ribs split and through the narrow slits, thousands of seeds, like black sawdust, sifted out into the breeze. The empty seed pod gamely held its head above the snow until, by early December, it had disappeared beneath the weight of winter.

As hard as I looked, I never found another pink lady's slipper on our land. I am not surprised, really. Orchids are the largest family of flowering plants, in the world: there are 25,000 species, two dozen of them native to northern Ontario. But the *Cypripedium*, the Lady's Slippers, are the most primitive. Reproduction is a delicate matter for them.

An orchid seed does not develop like other plant seeds. It is too tiny to carry much nutritional baggage. When it lands on moist soil and germinates, it swells to a minuscule corm. And that is as far as it goes. The protocorm does not grow into a lady's slipper unless the germinated seed is joined by a soil fungus in the genus *Rhizoctonia*. It isn't in a hurry — it can wait for up to two years — but without the fungus, there is no offspring.

The fungus and the seed live in symbiosis, but like many marriages, it is a precarious partnership, right from the start. The fungus originally seeks out the orchid seed to feed on its pathetically limited reserves of oil and protein. The orchid embryo, for its part, counterattacks, and starts to digest the fungus. Sometimes the fungus destroys the seed and sometimes the seed devours the fungus, but when conditions are right, the adversaries establish a delicate, mutually beneficial relationship, the fungus living off the outer tissues of the embryo while the orchid feeds off the parts of the fungus that penetrate deeper inside. Even after the seed and fungus set up housekeeping together, however, several seasons may pass before an orchid flowers. The *Cypripedium* apparently holds the record: it can take up to seventeen years to bring forth its first bloom.

Because of its delicate living arrangements — the fungi continue to help mature orchids absorb food from the soil — the lady's slipper cannot be transplanted. So, when I left Stonehill Acres, and my marriage of seventeen years, I left the lady's slipper behind. It has been four springs and still, during the first days of May, I am driven to look for the tender green shoots of my orchid. I never stop yearning for the cold grey granite that never flinches under my foot, as the limestone in this new place does. And I always think with longing of the weedy balsam firs and their tentative toehold in that indifferent place. But it is the lady's slipper I miss the most. I think now that I liked her so well because she survived on so little.

Before I left the north, I walked with my husband to the little hollow in the granite and pointed out to him the exact patch of moss where the lady's slipper would make her appearance. I recently heard that he has raised a building on that flat stretch of rock, that a car drives across that uplifted stone shoulder. Perhaps he forgot about the pink lady's slipper. Or perhaps he has learned other ways of making the landscape his own.

Gardens

Emily Carr
(1871 – 1945)

Emily Carr is well known as one of Canada's most famous painters whose work meditates on the nature of Canada's west coast. As well, she produced five books of stories and reminiscences, two of which, The Book of Small *(1942) and* Growing Pains *(1946), are represented in this anthology. Although Carr always kept journals, these books were written later in her life when poor health curtailed her painting. In the books, all of which are autobiographical, she recounts events charged with the heightened light of memory. The connection between nature and remembrance is an important one, for often the environment serves as a catalyst to recollecting and recapturing the past.* The Book of Small *concerns earliest events and is so named because, as the youngest child but one in the family, Carr was known as "Small."*

White Currants

from *The Book of Small* (1942)

It happened many times, and it always happened just in that corner of the old garden.

When it was going to happen, the dance in your feet took you there without your doing anything about it. You danced through the flower garden and the vegetable garden till you came to the row of currant bushes, and then you danced down it.

First came the black currants with their strong wild smell. Then came the red currants hanging in bright tart clusters. On the very last bush in the row the currants were white. The white currants ripened first. The riper they got, the clearer they grew, till you could almost see right through them. You could see the tiny veins in their skins and the seeds and the juice. Each currant hung there like an almost-told secret.

Oh! you thought, if the currants were just a wee bit clearer, then perhaps you could see them living, inside. The white currant bush was the finish of the garden, and after it was a little spare place before you came to the fence. Nobody ever came there except to dump garden rubbish.

Bursting higgledy-piggledy up through the rubbish everywhere, grew a half-wild mauvy-pink flower. The leaves and the blossoms were not much to look at, because it poured every drop of its glory into its smell. When you went there the colour and the smell took you and wrapped you up in themselves.

The smell called the bees and the butterflies from ever so far. The white butterflies liked it best; there were millions of them flickering among the pink flowers, and the hum of the bees never stopped.

The sun dazzled the butterflies' wings and called the smell out of the flowers. Everything trembled. When you went in among the mauvy-pink

178

flowers and the butterflies you began to tremble too; you seemed to become a part of it — and then what do you think happened? Somebody else was there too. He was on a white horse and he had brought another white horse for me.

We flew round and round in and out among the mauvy-pink blossoms, on the white horses. I never saw the boy; he was there and I knew his name, but who gave it to him or where he came from I did not know. He was different from other boys, you did not have to see him, that was why I liked him so. I never saw the horses either, but I knew that they were there and that they were white.

In and out, round and round we went. Some of the pink flowers were above our heads with bits of blue sky peeping through, and below us was a mass of pink. None of the flowers seemed quite joined to the earth — you only saw their tops, not where they went into the earth.

Everything was going so fast — the butterflies' wings, the pink flowers, the hum and the smell, that they stopped being four things and became one most lovely thing, and the little boy and the white horses and I were in the middle of it, like the seeds that you saw dimly inside the white currants. In fact, the beautiful thing was like the white currants, like a big splendid secret getting clearer and clearer every moment — just a second more and —

"Come and gather the white currants," a grown-up voice called from the vegetable garden.

The most beautiful thing fell apart. The bees and the butterflies and the mauvy-pink flowers and the smell, stopped being one and sat down in their own four places. The boy and the horses were gone.

The grown-up was picking beans. I took the glass dish.

"If we left the white currants, wouldn't they ripen a little more? Wouldn't they get — clearer?"

"No, they would shrivel."

"Oh!"

Then I asked, "What is the name of that mauvy-pink flower?"

"Rocket."

"Rocket?"

"Yes — the same as fireworks."

Rockets! Beautiful things that tear up into the air and burst!

Midge Ellis Keeble
(1914 –)

Midge Ellis Keeble wrote Tottering in My Garden *as the record for her children and friends of forty years of experience in six different gardens. When the price of photocopying the manuscript proved too costly the text was shown to a publisher and within a year the book became an instant classic of gardening fact and lore. The book is a useful guide to gardening but more importantly it is an enchanting and hilarious account of a life lived with (not against) nature.*

Birds, Bees and Other Weirds

from *Tottering in My Garden:*
A Gardener's Memoir with Notes for the Novice (1989)

Birds

One of the first things you'll do on coming to the country is buy a bird book. I like the *Audubon Society Field Guide*, but look them all over. I also have some of the Bent Life Histories Series, on the birds that concern me; he gives their lives in excruciating detail. Colin Harrison's *Field Guide to Nests, Eggs and Nestlings* is interesting. You can get carried away on this subject. You'll need a pair of good binoculars too. Then you'll put up a birdfeeding station close to the house and spend next spring weeding sunflowers out of the rose bed. Try to station it in a tree, set in the grass away from flower beds and near shrubs.

Winter is lovely. That is when the birds bring life to an otherwise bleak and still landscape. Brilliant blue jays, purple finches, scarlet cardinals all hob-nob with the neat little juncos and chickadees. The downy woodpecker swings crazily about, upside down on a suet ball. The mourning doves (and, to my annoyance, someone's matched pairs of pigeons) perambulate with great self-importance on the ground, though nothing is as stately as the big black crows in spring; they look solemn as undertakers. The real joy for us this far north is the snow buntings. They come in flocks of fifty, wheeling in unison, attached by an invisible web. They're white with a thin brown stripe on head and wing. One winter day as the sun was setting, a flock settled all facing one way in the locust tree. The sun changed the brown stripe to gold and there they were, each wearing a thin gold circlet on its head. Enchanted princesses, obviously, straight out of *Giselle*.

Spring comes and the problems start. If ever you wondered where "bird-brain," "feather-brain," or "airhead" came from, you have only to watch a mother bird in action. They keep losing their kids. When they find them, they carry on as if it were the baby's fault. If you put the baby back in the nest, it promptly falls out again and now the mother won't touch it because you did.

I spent a harrowing two days, three years ago, when a swallow built her nest on the barn beam crossing under the roof of the pool-house. Now we couldn't use the pool-house and had to sit out on the deck, well to one side.

From there I watched the proceedings. Four heads with open beaks were visible. Mama flew in and out, stuffing food into the beak on the left. I couldn't believe it. None of the "one for you and one for you" stuff. The biggest beak and the longest neck got it all.

I remonstrated, "How about the little fellow on the right?" Perhaps they shifted around, but not while I was watching. However, when the time came for them to fly away, all four wheeled off into the sky.

Two more heads appeared. All this time they'd been underneath, trampled by their siblings and getting nary a bite. They were very small, very weak and scared out of their teeny-tiny wits. Mama didn't feed them. She urged them up until they were teetering on the edge of the nest. Then she nagged and nagged them to fly. They were terrified.

By now I was beside myself and found myself calling a bird a bird-brain. "Feed them!"

The rest of the story is very sad. The first baby fell to the deck. I attended his funeral. The second managed to get his wings open before he hit the deck and spent two days staggering around, wings outspread, but couldn't take off. I abandoned everything and baby-sat for two days, keeping him out of the pool, but he managed to drown himself at dawn before I was up. And if you think I'm weird, you should hear what some of my friends have gone through. Sometimes I just can't stand birds.

But there are birds and there are birds. A pair of eastern blue-birds ignored our nesting boxes and raised their young deep in a north shrubbery, against all the rules. They are supposed to prefer a box, out in the open, facing south. (Well, they hadn't read the book.) One a lovely summer day the parents stationed themselves about eight feet apart in two apple trees. The two babies then went through a "Fly to Mummy, now fly to Daddy" routine back and forth, practising landings and take-offs, while four of us sat on the steps, afraid to breathe. It went on for an hour and we will never understand that one. Obviously the babies had flown from the nesting site to the apple tree; so why all the practice? A pair of caring parents.

Just like snowflakes, no two birds are alike. I discovered this when a wood thrush burst into song in the red maple tree. His song filled the garden, the magnificent tone soared to the sky. A Pavarotti of a bird! Praying he would never stop, I stayed to the very end. For the next few days I kept an eye out for him, and at last there he was, in the same tree and almost the same branch, I waited. He sang. It wasn't the same bird. It was the same song, very pretty, but he didn't have the chest, the arch to the beak, the great chambers in his little skull for resonance. And you know, he didn't give a damn? He sang anyway. It seemed only polite to hear him out and, as he threw all his heart and soul into it, I found it difficult to decide which bird I admired more.

Should you think I exaggerate, I have witnesses. Ro and her husband John recently bought and refurbished a beautiful old farmhouse just a mile up the line. It was meant for weekends, but in May they decided to try country living full time. Early one morning, Ro called. Did I have a bird book?

"This bird ... it sang ... you've never heard ... you can't believe ... "

"Yes, I can. It was a thrush."

"Its beak was straight and its colour was — oh I couldn't see — if you could have heard ... "

By now I had my *Audubon Field Guide* in hand, turned to page 667. "Ro? Here it is. Now listen carefully. This is what Thoreau had to say. 'Whenever a man hears it he is young, and Nature is in her spring; where he hears it, it is a new world and a free country, and the gates of heaven are not shut against him.' "

All I could hear was Ro softly breathing.

"That it?"

She managed to say yes, very quietly.

"There you are then. It was a wood thrush," and I gently replaced the receiver, leaving her to contemplate the wonders of country living, in a garden, in the spring.

Bees

I know I shouldn't get into this. It really is weird, and what is more, I don't understand it. Long ago I settled myself with a book and a cool drink in the Sand Garden, waiting for the train to go by. No sooner settled than a bee dived at my ear, then my nose. I got up and walked about and he followed. I sat again and there he was. Why I should have remembered at that moment that my English grandmother "told the bees" I don't know. In her part of Shropshire, if there was a birth, death or wedding (and that was just about all the excitement there was) the lady of the house went to the hives and "told the bees."

I contemplated the pesky creature in front of me. There was no one around. So I told it, "No one's been born, died or married that I know of, but here's the family news in brief." He flew away.

Nancy C. joined me some days later and so did the bee. "That thing is driving my [sic] crazy," she said. I told her what I had tried and Nancy, an unbeliever if ever there was one, looked at it and said crisply, "The news hasn't changed since the last time." It flew away and neither of us cared to comment.

Years and years passed during which I held no further conversations with bees. Then we come to the country garden and more years pass. The Canterbury bells had gone off and had to be cut, so I went out with my flower cutters and couldn't get at them for bees. There's no one around in the country and you can find yourself talking to everything from the cat to the cows, so thoughtlessly I remarked, "Why can't you move to the borage? You like that," and, giving up, turned away to find something else to snip. When I turned back they were all on the borage. Three or four, too groggy to move, lingered on, deep in a bell. I cut those down carefully and swathed down the rest, wondering. It doesn't makes sense, you see. People who spend their lives in research on bees will tell you that a single bee is not really an individual. The swarm is the individual. Yet talking to one bee had worked too. Do bees have ears? Well, you will agree that it's strange. I will confess that, if I am absolutely sure no one can possibly hear me, I will talk to a bee; so I should no doubt add myself to the list of weirds.

The Racing Charolais

We do not keep animals. But Harold and Dot, who had a large barn and a large field, felt they should really get into the country living style. They started with two horses. That was a lovely interlude. We could see them, manes flying, galloping from here to there in the distant field. But, deciding they wanted something quieter and only the best, they sold the horses and acquired six Charolais cows.

Sunday morning we were at the toast stage when Harold pounded on the kitchen door. Agonized and apologetic, he told us that the cows were loose somewhere on our property and would trample down the garden. Dot ran up and called to me, "Get a rake!" I got the rake. What was I supposed to do with it? We organized: Harold's daughter Cindy took off north in the jeep, Dot took off in the station wagon, heading west, and Harold and Gordon started down along the fence into the woods.

"You stand on guard," they said and left me all alone in the morning sunshine. At last I found out what the rake was for. If you set it, prongs down, on the grass and wrap an arm around the handle, it makes a nice thing to lean on while you warm your bones in the sun and munch your toast. Ages passed. Aeons passed. I gazed out at the far fields. A funny-looking red-gold ball was coming out of the woods into Harold's field. There was another. The balls had four legs. The Charolais were back in their own field and there was no one to tell.

The cows circumnavigated our property in this wise every Sunday morning (Cindy's beau was leaving the gate open every Saturday night). Then the inevitable happened; he left our gate open as well. Instead of turning sharp left and coming up our drive, the cows turned sharp right, out through our gate and moved briskly onto the 7th line. They were seen, moving at a fast trot, heading for the Airport Road. Going south, and now very inspirited by passing cars, they cantered to the flashing light, turning on to the Peel County Road and, when they came to Highway 10, took the home stretch at a full gallop with everyone in hot pursuit. Then they saw a lush green field and dashed in, and the farmer ran to the gate and locked it.

All interested parties gathered in the field. The farmer turned to Harold. "Those are fine beasts."

"Yes, they are," said Harold.

"A little thin."

"Well, they run a lot."

After further exchanges, a deal was struck, and the Charolais settled into their new home. "It was either that or enter them at Woodbine race-track," said Harold. Cindy found a new beau.

Miranda

We were urged by one and all to (a) keep chickens, (b) fatten cows, (c) build a pond and buy ducks, but we were content to share in our friends' amazing adventures. We had all the animals we wanted in the woods. They took care of themselves and wandered out to visit when the mood struck them. And we had Miranda. In the early days, she got herself talked about.

"That cat is wearing eye-liner."

"And bangs. Bangs?"

"Who does she think she is — Marilyn Monroe?"

You may guess she was not all that popular with the ladies, but men would cuddle her up and purr along with her, "You should just feel this cat's coat." All of which sounds as though she devoted her time to being ornamental but we knew just how hard she worked for her living. At first there was a slight problem of territory. In the first week she had disap-peared overnight and in the morning I went out to the top of the hill, sending a clarion call: Miraaandaaa! This had always brought her lolloping home, but not this time. For the sake of the neighbours, the calling and hallooing had to be spaced out, and after an hour I decided I would have to search along the roads; but just as I got to the top of the driveway I could see coming in at the gate one small, very, very tired cat. She tried to run, gave up, and just lay down on the gravel, so I carried her home. After that, nothing would persuade her to walk out through the gate or into the woods. We were accompanied on all walks around the property, but at the gate or the woods she would sit down firmly and wait for us to come back.

Now, with her own boundaries staked out in her head, she went to work. No mice. Our mice are really voles and some of them are full of fight. Her nose was scratched, her paw bitten, but she battled on to clear the garden of all voles, an impossible task. Suitors came to call, unaware that after her visit to the vet, she just wasn't interested. The fur would fly, and one morning, finding huge tufts of white fur all over the terrace, we realized that Barbara's tom must be walking around in his skin. I phoned to apologize, but Barbara just said, "Serves him right." When a neighbour's dog came over the hill, Miranda dropped belly to ground, clawed her way through the grass toward him, the front hissing and spitting like a small steam engine and the caboose twitching with tail swinging back and forth. The dog froze in amazement, then turned and ran. Groundhogs she never figured out. She would drop to the ground and stare. The groundhog would stare. They never got closer than two yards. The staring match would go on and then, as though by mutual agreement, they would both turn and walk away.

But the birds? What were we to do about the birds? We decided the first time she caught one we would have to get her a collar with a bell. I was sunning on the front porch when she came in, tail proudly erect, bringing me a live brown thrasher held lightly in her mouth, for all the world like a retriever. I am ashamed to say I smacked her hard, jumping up and down and yelling, "No! No birds!" Her mouth opened and the bird flew off unharmed. I sat down again on the porch and Miranda approached, looking more puzzled than offended. She patted my knee with her paw to get attention. I tried to explain, "Birds? No. Mice? Yes. I'm sorry I hit you, Miranda, but no birds. Birds are out." Then I came to and realized I was talking to a cat. We looked for and couldn't find a bell that would fit a cat. But as the hunt went on we came to realize we wouldn't need it — she wasn't catching birds. She would chitter at them, watch them closely and switch her tail, then sigh and go off to look for a mouse.

Howard and Bob, who had come to paint the house, explained the whole thing. "She can talk." She certainly made a lot of strange noises, but talk? All I knew was that the three of them would sit out in the sun at noon hour, holding long conversations while she ate all the chicken in their sandwiches.

Was she a cat? We weren't all that sure. If she could talk and wouldn't catch birds? She was just Miranda — a little weird.

Stephanie Quainton Steel
(1935 –)

In Harvest of Light, *Stephanie Quainton Steel explores the connections among nature, art and writing. After she took up kayaking (despite her fear of water!) Steele was free to pursue her life-long passion for the west coast of British Columbia which her grandparents pioneered at the turn of the century. Through her travels she sought the solitude and historical roots to her own story as a person, writer and artist.* Harvest of Light *is also a plea for preserving wilderness places as sanctuaries for future generations.*

Salal Joe's Garden

from *Harvest of Light: An Artist's Journey* (1991)

Overhead black clouds filled the sky and far-off thunder rattled the hills. It was obvious my latest Barkley Sound excursion was thwarted for now. *Raven Moon* sat in dry dock on the roof racks of my car, a nylon cover crimped tight like a chef's cap to the cockpit to keep out the rain. I huddled inside the car with my gear. If I could bear one night of such tight quarters, perhaps morning would be fine enough for me to leave shore with my camping gear still dry. My plan for this trip was to bestow upon Turret Island some seedlings of mint and cress that I had tucked away amongst my gear. I hoped to start a crop of herbs that I might harvest for salad and tea on future trips.

I collapsed the back seat of the Scirrocco and unrolled my sleeping bag. As I wormed my way inside, I could hear occasional rumblings of the thunder, but in a short time it seemed to have retreated to the slopes far away, while the mist moved silently past the hills looking for new valleys to haunt.

At least I was dry. I lay listening to the staccato of rain on the roof and on *Raven Moon*. Sleep did not come easily. I even thought about heading out in the unsettled weather. I felt strangely wide awake, energized, perhaps, by the ions in the air.

I tried to concentrate on Barkley Sound in the hope that pleasant thoughts would have a soporific effect and lull me off to sleep. My mind drifted to a story a friend had told me about a reclusive man who had been a squatter in Barkley Sound. Salal Joe, as he was known, had been there when the islands had become part of Pacific Rim National Park in the 1970s and had been allowed to remain under the tradition of squatter's rights. Joe was a reaper of the branches of that plant's shiny green leaves, and an eater of the wild purple-black berries that grew on the southeastern sides of the islands in the Broken Group. He made the small income he required selling salal to the Vancouver Island florist shops.

Salal Joe lived on a floating raft and spent his time foraging among the islands in a small wooden dinghy. On Dodd Island he had established a quite remarkable garden. Not content just to grow essentials, Joe had planted not only a cherry tree, a plum tree and an apple tree, but also a rosebush, a mountain ash and a great clump of bamboo.

When the small island deer began to nibble off bits of tree bark and the roses from his bushes, he went off scrounging the beaches until he found some great fishnets. These he dragged home half in and half out of the dinghy, a job that must have taken days. Then he put up driftwood posts, secured the netting with bits of scrounged rope and made a gate out of beach-worn wood. At last he closed his garden to all save the insects and birds.

Salal Joe had an abiding love for the area and it must have been alarming to find the very first park visitors — and there were not many back then — come drifting up to his floathouse to ask directions or just to chat. Joe became a well-known character to those who visited the area. And if they came back to the islands in another year, they would find he hadn't changed; he was just as peculiar as ever. Joe claimed he had escaped from Russia, where he was suspected of being a spy, and always added that he didn't mind. In fact, he would say, he was quite likely just going to disappear someday. He'd be gone to lie on the beaches soaking up the sun in California.

And then early one season an upturned boat was discovered banging against the logs on one of the islands at high tide. Closer investigation proved what the park superintendent had feared. It was Salal Joe's dinghy.

A search was instigated, starting at the float houses on Turtle Island and continuing around Dodd Island. Here the gate to the garden was found swinging in the afternoon wind. That was unusual! Joe always kept the gate latched. Perhaps it was an oversight, but was there a connection? Had he hurried away from the garden for some reason? Had he got caught in one of those southwest winds? They often got up fast, in ten minutes, first with patches of gooseflesh on the water, and then calm again, and then the onslaught like a broom rushing down through the channels to sweep everything out toward the open sea.

After several days park officials really began to fear the worst, but a search of both high tides and low produced not a trace.

Did anyone know if Joe had been able to swim? Nobody could answer. No one wanted to accept the possibility that a sudden wind had swept him from his boat. They decided that Joe, true to his word, had gone off to the beaches of California. And so the search was stopped.

The floathouse remained a derelict. One of the park officials kindly latched up the garden gate, and with that latching, Joe faded into the folklore of the past.

My recollection of the Salal Joe story put me off to sleep at last. Though I tossed and turned several times during the night, I slept through and awoke with relief to find the mountains silent, clear and cloudless.

If only I had more time, I thought, during my three-day stay, perhaps I could have fitted in a stop on Dodd Island to look for Salal Joe's garden. But if I did that as a side trip, I would thwart my original plan to go around the outside coast and look for the cave on Dicebox Island.

Deciding to stick with my first intention, I set out directly to Turret Island. There I surveyed the local stream for a suitable planting spot for the mint and cress. It was disappointing to find the scene quite different than the image I had carried in my mind of a green wood and freckled sunlight. The place by the stream was brown and dark, the tall hemlocks oppressive. There was very little light, and the rapidly drying pools were covered in the oily scum so typical of centuries of piled-up conifer needles. It was unlikely that mint and cress would survive in such a place; my plan had been only the fantasy of a hungry winter mind. Nevertheless, I would plant some anyway, but save the best of the plants in the hope of finding a more suitable location. I rummaged in my boat, but found as I hunted high and low, muttering under my breath as I pulled out packet after packet of my food supplies until everything lay in a heap on the beach, that there was nothing resembling either mint or cress anywhere amongst my supplies. At last I came to the conclusion that my plant packages were still sitting on the steps at home where I had placed my gear ready for loading.

After three attempts to find the missing plants, I looked up to find that the rose and pink of morning had now levelled a finger of strong wind down the channels between the islands. It was not going to be the best weather for Dicebox Island after all. I could get trapped there, perhaps for days, by bad weather. Even Turret Island was too exposed. I must reorganize my trip plans. Within half an hour I had repacked my gear and was heading off to find a campsite on a more protected island.

As I paddled *Raven Moon* down the length of Turret Island the wind freshened, and I soon found myself in a losing battle to maintain my course. I flew past Turtle Island all in a rush. Was it the wind that turned my boat toward Dodd Island?

That's not a bad idea after all, I thought, and stopped fighting *Raven Moon* for control. Why not adapt to the second plan and go to see if I could find Salal Joe's garden?

Raven Moon, once she had her head, behaved like an unruly horse. She seemed to know full well her capabilities in rough seas. As I backbraced just to keep her balanced, she nosed her way along and Dodd Island loomed up dead ahead. She took me straight ashore.

As soon as she nudged the beach, I leapt out and dragged her free of the dumping waves, up over the kelp and the drifted logs until she was securely above the tides. Stepping back to breathe myself free of the exertion, I looked up to take my bearings. Directly above me was a square of boards and fishnets. Salal Joe's garden!

Thoughts of the open coast disappeared. I could find a more appropriate camping ground later, when the wind dropped. For now I wanted to see why Salal Joe had chosen this island over all the others for his garden.

Salal Joe had been missing now for four years, and I found the path he had made was rapidly disintegrating. New growth obliterated most of the early marks, but the imposing height of upended beach logs covered in plastic netting strangely had no look of decay about it at all.

Construction of this garrison must have been a monumental task, and the determination to create a safe spot for growing plants must have been of supreme importance for the man to have laboured with a fence so heavy and so permanent. It stood above my head by a good two feet. I could not see to the inside for the thickness of its layers against the boards, but I could see trees, trees that were nothing like the varieties found in the forest. These had large lacings of leaves that clattered together, making their own special music in the wind.

I approached the closed gate, hand outstretched. Then I remembered my friend's comment about the park officials who had found it unlatched and almost symbolically had done it up. It seemed a strange gesture, almost as if with the latching of a gate one could contain the essence of the strange man who had created the place, that maybe never would the inside of this garden decay so long as the outside was not let in.

A group of crows distracted my thoughts as they began cackling in the forest beside me. Were they sending me warnings? I looked up at them in the branches of the hemlocks above me and clicked my tongue noisily to make them flap off down the beach to continue their racket out of my way.

I realized suddenly that I had dropped the gate latch during the noisy intrusion. I quickly put out my hand. As I grasped it again the crows flew back to chide me once more. In a moment of irritation I decided to ignore them; I would see the garden whether the crows or the gate approved or not. Taking hold of the latch, I pushed against a resistant layer of grass. With a creaking of old bones it yielded to my strength. I took a step into another world ...

You could tell the place had once burgeoned and blossomed. Everything had grown in a crazy, rampant way. There was the cherry tree, the mountain ash, the plum and the apple tree, and in one corner beside a clump of strange-looking bamboo, a rose had straggled over and become bound with creeping wild vines. The whole garden had a weedy growth wrapping it round in a wild tangle. The precious plants of Salal Joe had struggled hard for territory and existence. Without his care the years had taken a sad toll; many had strangled. Yet there was a mystique about the garden, a reverence that was part of the air within it. I found I wanted to sit down in spite of the mosquitoes that rose up from the long grass to feast upon any exposed flesh they could find. I wanted to sit, and as the artist Gauguin had said about art as abstraction, *derive the abstraction from Nature while dreaming before it*.

I chose a spot under the cherry tree, leaned my back against its trunk and for only a moment closed my eyes. It was good to rest after the toil of the morning in a place where the wind seemed absent. I felt my tired body relax; a deep peace began settling into my bones.

Suddenly my body gave a twitch. I opened my eyes and found myself staring at a huge forest slug as big as a cigar. I could see the slug's eyes out on stalks that moved up and down, this way and that, as if feeling the air while it oozed its way up the stem of the rosebush, looking for decayed matter to eat. All around the slug were the skeletons of eaten leaves.

Other bugs came into my vision, too, now that I was sitting still, slugs and centipedes. I sat quietly watching them munching away at the tender shoots of plants that were not natives of the place but had been brought there by loving hands to grow in the peace of the forested island. They had taken on an air of the exotic, a culinary speciality in the world of insects.

I suddenly felt vaguely uneasy. The peace and tranquillity that had overtaken me disappeared as quickly as they had come. Somewhere nearby the crows resumed their clattering cacophony.

I got to my feet, uncomfortable now, and hurried out of the garden. In a moment of respect for Salal Joe, I heaved the gate shut as I passed.

The crows flapped away in alarm. I ran down onto the beach, a strong feeling of apprehension hot on my heels, though I didn't know why. What time was it? To my horror I discovered the tide had come in while I was gone. And there was no sign of *Raven Moon*!

Frantic, I ran to the point of land that jutted from the corner of the island. How long had I slept? There was no sign of my kayak anywhere. I ran along the beach to the first point, then crossed the isthmus and back. I ran the other way until steep rocks stopped my passage. Anguish pushed all my blood to my brain. What was I to do now? I slumped down in a lump on the beach stones and shed tears of abject frustration. What now?

It was some time before the first glimmerings of reason began to filter back. I could wait it out; perhaps someone would come by, another kayaker, boaters perhaps. But this was only May, I realized. I had deliberately chosen to come out of season when there was unlikely to be another soul in the area. I looked out to sea. The distant specks along the horizon were only islands and more islands, each wild and lonely and covered in trees. I had become the only human on earth and ocean.

I walked dejectedly back across the shore. At least I had taken my gear out of the boat. At least I had done that; but I bitterly regretted not having realized that *Raven Moon* was my only lifeline to civilization. I had been careless. I had not secured her. She had been intractable all day, and now she was gone.

There was little I could do about it, so I occupied myself with setting up my tent. With the food I had brought I would be comfortable for several days before hunger became a serious threat. There would, of course, be seafood after that, so I would not starve. Water, though, might pose a different problem. In my canteen I had only enough, if rationed, for three or four days at most. Zipped inside my tent, I could light the little candle for the dark. It might last two days — some comfort ...

But what about *Raven Moon*? I counted out the approximate hours till tide change, knowing with incredible hindsight that I hadn't even brought the tide book for local waters, only my charts. What were my chances of finding *Raven Moon* further around the island as soon as the next low tide allowed me to get along the beach? It was a glimmer of hope — perhaps she had only drifted a beach or two away. After all, she had wanted to come here in the first place, hadn't she? What were my chances the next rising tide might just wash her back to this same beach? Now that's too much, I thought — a chance that was less than remote. I cursed myself for not having brought a flashlight so that I could search if the tide went out during the night. Most of all, I cursed *Raven Moon* for her betrayal.

With one of thirteen matches I built a roaring fire and got out my camp billy, thinking that food would cheer me up. Inside my cooking pot when I opened it were some Ziploc bags. Inside these were the packages of cress and mint that I thought I had left at home in Deep Cove. They had been with me all along!

I quickly opened the bag so the plants could breathe and then set about making a big stew in the pot. After dinner I would do something about them. Finding the plants made me feel much more cheerful. Maybe I wasn't so stupid after all. I would buck up and do the best I could.

I sat down to my repast, but, as I poked down mouthfuls that tasted like paper, I couldn't help thinking of my treasured boat being salvaged on distant shores by callous mariners.

When my plate was empty I set about searching for trails that might lead to the hidden beaches of the island. The first one I found led through high patches of salal, which I pushed out of my way as I went, noting that at some time long ago there had been a well-cut path. Suddenly I was out on the beach again. The island had an unexpectedly narrow isthmus hidden by dense groves of salal. Down the beach was a small lagoon and what looked like a freshwater stream.

No wonder Salal Joe had liked this island! It was simply beautiful in the real sense: a horseshoe bay of small cobblestones, driftwood whitened by long exposure to the sun along the half circle, marsh grass hedging the banks of the purling brown stream that spilled out of the bush and snaked its way to sea. Windfallen trees crossed the narrow inlet in three or four places, making it possible for me to cross back and forth over the stream. I tasted the water above the beach and found it was fresh and sweet. I began to look for a grassy pocket of growing soil; it was time to plant the mint and cress.

Returning quickly to my camp, I fetched the bags with their green and precious cargo, then kneeling down, a little like a suppliant at prayer for my good fortune at being still well and safe on shore, I cupped my hands and pulled up in each a lump of the peat-like earth, tucked in the plant shoots and tamped them down.

Overhead, crows moved silently into my awareness again. They had stopped scolding, but I felt they were keeping an eye on me with concentrated curiosity. I caught glimpses of their iridescent black shadow shapes drifting from limb to limb above me. I wondered if they carried some of the essence of the legendary gardener of Dodd Island.

Now that I had completed my chore, I suddenly felt a lightened mood. It wasn't so bad to be a castaway. I thought of Robinson Crusoe. This might have been a choice place to live. There were berries and green food. There was water, and there was the garden.

I soon shrugged it off. It's crazy, I thought. I can want this kind of life a lot, but circumstance has already given me a very different script. I am an artist, and I need the stimulation of life near a village with other people around, with libraries, bookstores, at least for part of the year. It was madness even to entertain the thought that I might be happy spending all my time on a quiet little island with ravens and crows — but what was it that Salal Joe threw away in favour of the hermit life? I kept asking myself.

It grew dark while I pondered the mystery of the strange inhabitant. The crows went to roost for the night. They totally accepted their life here on the island, while I continued to think of all that was valuable in the choice I had made when I bought land in Deep Cove.

I decided not to worry, not yet; a boat would come eventually. My housesitter, after waiting an extra day or two for the chance of bad weather making it impossible for me to be on time, would send out the alarm.

I returned to my tent just before it was too dark to see. There I packed everything for the night. I made one last desperate check of the beach in a vain hope of recovering my recalcitrant boat. Then I lit my candle and crawled inside the tent and into my night attire, first my woolies, then my sleeping bag. This would not be a bad life, I told myself again as I warmed up in the comfort of the nest I had made.

I'm not sure when in the night Salal Joe made his appearance, but I somehow knew that he would come. I had long been told that creatures from the spirit world would not harm me. I had made the decision not to sit up wasting rationed midnight wax to keep a ghost away.

First there was much crackling of the dry mossy undergrowth near my tent; then I heard footfalls too loud for mice. Though I never lifted the tent flap, I began to see him standing outside. I noticed suddenly that he was reaching out toward me, that he held something in his hand. Something that glinted in the moonlight now speckling among the trees. A shiny object. I stared out through the mosquito netting. Yes, it was a stick, old, shiny with hand rubbing — a digging stick like the Indians used.

A hot feeling speared down through the centre of me. Salal Joe actually wanted me to take the stick; he kept reaching out with it. I pulled a trembling hand from the warmth of the sleeping bag and, removing the mosquito curtain that stood between us, I reached and took the smooth old stick from the cold night air.

At once the apparition vanished. I stared out at the low slung cedar branches moving gently in the breath of the night ...

There was no breeze in the morning. It was quiet and still; mist moved softly over the water. I prepared my granola, but did not have the usual enthusiasm for camp food. I knew I should have felt at ease and glad that morning had come, that things were getting warm, but a vague uneasiness rattled me. It was as if there were something I had left undone.

I recalled the dream — but it hadn't been a dream! I had been wide awake when the bushes had crackled. I had seen the strange man at my tent door. Even the mice had stopped scuttling when the apparition had visited camp. And he had brought me something, had handed it to me before I had scared him away.

I put down my food and hurried to the tent. I fumbled around the sides of my sleeping bag. Yes, there it was — a digging stick, like the Indians used. That was it! Of course!

I left the breakfast I was eating for the mice to enjoy; I had had enough. There was so much to do today! I hurried over to the fishnet and log fence. Quickly I undid the gate latch and entered the garden.

Hours passed. My hands turned black from the rich midden soil as I set to weeding and clearing out the choking roots that had overtaken the garden plot. When at last I knelt up from my toil, all that survived of Salal Joe's plants were clear of weeds, even the rosebush. And as if to reward me, I discovered buds on it that had been hidden by stifling wild vines. It would bloom now. That must have been what Salal Joe had wanted, to see the garden blossom ...

The job done, I knelt back and looked up above the high netting into the hemlock trees. Then I caught a glimpse through the fishnet mesh of the jungle of salal pressing ever closer toward the fence as time went by. I saw the small flock of island crows watching me quizzically from low-hanging branches.

"There, it's done," I said aloud, knowing suddenly as I said it that I was now free from the spell of the island. The crows stared back at me, not making their usual racket, but staring silently.

I stood up and once more admired Salal Joe's wonderful garden. Yes, I thought, one could live here all right. Living this way would have all kinds of rewards. I backed out of the garden very quietly and latched the gate behind me. The crows went off down the beach to hunt for clams.

It was time to go. I looked down the shore and smiled at *Raven Moon* where she rested on the mark of the high tide.

For the Future

Alexandra Morton
(1957 –)

*Alexandra Morton lives in Simoom Sound on Gilford Island,
British Columbia with her son Jarret and her daughter Clio. Known as
"the Whale Lady," she is part of a network of marine biologists who
observe and record the life of whales off the coast of British Columbia.
In addition to this research work, she is a writer and artist. Her first
children's book,* Siwiti — A Whale's Story *(1991), won the
Sheila A. Egoff Children's Book Prize.* In the Company of Whales
*introduces young people to the techniques of natural history and the
biology of whales but more importantly, like all nature writing, it seeks
to inspire wonder and respect in the reader.* In the Company of
Whales *was awarded the 1995 KIND Book Award by the National
Association for Humane and Enviromental Education.*

Introduction

from *In the Company of Whales* (1993)

When I first arrived in British Columbia I did not expect to spend the rest of my life here. My intention was to visit for a few summers, study whales and return each winter to a job in a city.

I had always liked the idea of living in the wilderness, but I had never actually experienced it, so there were many surprises. All the beautiful films and pictures didn't prepare me for how itchy, soggy and dirty it could be. But from the first day I arrived, I was sure that I had finally found my place on this planet. I cannot explain why, but, after travelling to many places, I just knew that this was where I wanted to stay. The reason I came to British Columbia was to find one particular family of killer whales; I stayed because I fell in love with the place.

The first killer whales or orca that I came across were in a small pool near Los Angeles. When I first met them I thought they were slow, uninteresting creatures. At that time, 1978, I was studying communication among the quick, playful, bottle-nosed dolphins in another tank at Marineland of the Pacific. I was trying to figure out their language and I thought a good way to do that might be to keep track of everything they did and every sound they made. Then on my computer I could match the two. As everyone knows, it is not easy to figure out what a person is saying in another language. It is even more difficult to figure out what another species is saying! The big trouble was that the eleven dolphins in that tank moved so fast I simply could not describe every move they made.

By comparison the killer whales seemed quite uninteresting. Whenever I happened to pass their tank, Orky, the male, was usually just floating on the surface, his flopped-over dorsal fin resembling an old car tire. The female, Corky, was always moving, circling the tank again and again. Some of the children who came to see her thought she was a machine because she always came up in the same spot to breathe. I never watched them for long.

Then one day Corky surprised all of us by having a baby. No one knew she was pregnant until the tiny tail of her calf appeared. The curator of the park asked me to bring my underwater listening equipment from the dolphin tank and record the sounds of the new baby. I was very happy to be asked and wondered what a baby killer whale would sound like. I was so interested I stayed awake for most of three days, napping in my chair whenever the whales were quiet, which was not often. Whales do not sleep like us and can stay awake all night. The baby made a raspy little cry that was not very different from a human baby's cry.

What I witnessed at the aquarium was very sad. Corky did not know how to take care of her baby. We guessed that she had not been old enough to learn how to be a mother before she was captured. The baby never nursed, though he tried.

Within a few days the little whale died. My home was two hours from the aquarium and I cried the whole way. But, as a result of this experience, I decided that the slower-moving killer whales would be easier to study than the dolphins. At least my eyes and mouth could keep up with them.

I spent two years studying Orky and Corky on a part-time basis. Every month I spent twelve hours watching them. One month I spent the day from 6 AM to 6 PM watching the whales and the next month I spent the night from 6 PM to 6 AM. I did this so I could find out if they did different things at night. I recorded their sounds and wrote down everything I saw.

I enjoyed being with the whales at night best because there were no other people around. They played whale games and were always up to something new. And they were certainly not at all boring! They did strange things I didn't understand, like greeting the sunrise with their mouths open and tongues stuck out!

At the end of the two years Corky had another baby and it died too. Watching baby whales die was too sad for me, so I decided to try studying whales in the wild.

Each family of killer whales speaks a slightly different language, called a dialect. No one knows why they do this, but some of us think it is so they don't get confused and lost when many families travel together. Imagine you are in a dark field with your family and a lot of other people. If there was something about your family's speech that set it apart from the rest, it would be easier for your mother or father to tell you when it was time to go. Underwater it is murky and often very dark, and it would be easy for a whale to get separated from its family.

Having spent two years learning Corky's family dialect, I didn't want to start all over again with a new language, so I decided to try and find her family. I knew that Dr. Mike Bigg, one of the top research scientists in the field, had counted and photographed almost all the families of whales on the west coast, so I called him. I was nervous because he was so famous and I was only twenty years old. I worried that he would think I was just a kid and not want to talk to me. But my fears were unfounded. Dr. Bigg was very nice and told me what I needed to know. He sent me pictures of Corky's family and said that the best place to look for them was off the east coast of Vancouver Island near Alert Bay during the month of August.

I spent the next few months making lists of what I would need for this exciting expedition. I saved enough money to buy an inflatable boat and practised going out in it. When the time came, I piled pots and pans, tent, boat, engine, food, tape recorder, camera, and lots of warm clothes into the back of my pickup truck. And off I went. It took me three days to drive from San Diego to Alert Bay.

Due to Dr. Bigg's help and lots of luck I found the whales I was looking for the very first day. In actual fact, they found me. I was still tied to the dock in Alert Bay when I heard them blowing. It was sunset and they looked very beautiful. The ocean was golden and their blows looked silver. It felt like the beginning of my life. I wished with all my heart that I could have brought Corky with me to see her family again.

I was raised in Connecticut in the mountains of New England, a place very different from the island I live on now. When I first moved here, there was a great deal I had to learn about the ocean and the forest. At first I was very brave. I didn't really know anything about the dangers involved, so I wasn't afraid. Then experience taught me otherwise. I felt the tremendous power of big storms on the ocean. I hit a rock and nearly sank my boat. One day a bear tried to push down the side of my house. When I first heard wolves howling at night, I thought for sure I was going to be attacked. And when my boat broke down in the middle of nowhere, I thought I was going to drift away and be lost forever. But out of fear comes respect, and I eventually learned to understand and respect the power of the natural environment.

Not long after I moved to Alert Bay I met Robin Morton, a filmmaker, and later we were married and began to work together. I felt very safe with Robin, because no matter how bad things got, he always figured out what to do. If the boat broke down, he fixed it. If we got lost, he found the way. I could generally just follow his instructions and take care of our baby.

Then one terrible afternoon Robin's diving equipment failed and he drowned. I did not know it was possible to feel that sad. I didn't want to talk to anybody or do anything. I didn't even want to get up in the morning. Fortunately there was one person who needed me. One person who made me get up and keep going and that was my son Jarret.

And so I had two choices. I could abandon my work and the life I had come to love, or I could learn to live independently with my son, who was four years old. I chose to stay where I was.

When I think back now to the many mistakes I made, I have to laugh. In the beginning I couldn't even split a piece of firewood properly. When the axe got stuck in a round of wood, I didn't know how to get it out and broke the handle. When I first used a chainsaw, I felt like I was holding a snarling beast by the tail and that at any second it might turn and rip my leg off. If a twig snapped in the bushes at night, I imagined a Sasquatch might be out there. I couldn't even manage to tie up my boat properly and it was lost in a storm, along with Jarret's Lego set. But two things helped me get through that part of my life: my neighbours and my love of the wilderness.

Someone taught me how to handle a chainsaw. I thought women weren't strong enough for this kind of thing, but when I saw that a friend, Joannie, could do it, I knew it was possible. Another person kept repairing my engine and finally I learned to do some of it myself. There is no electricity where we live, so I had to learn how to keep a generator running as well. I was shown how to fire a rifle, and while I have never had to use it, I no longer have to fear bears pushing down the side of my house. Everyone laughed at me for being afraid of wolves, so I gave that up. Storms still scare me on the water, but I go out anyway. I have learned to watch the weather, trying to read the clouds and water, so I know when to head for shelter. Because of my experiences, I now feel that I can handle most of what comes my way. And if I can't, I ask for help.

Jarret has grown up in the wilderness. I know I would have liked to have lived here when I was a child. When he was born, his father and I lived on a boat. Many people said that was no place to raise a child, but Jarret thought it was great. All the furniture was nailed to the floor, so he never had to worry about breaking things. And everywhere we went he had all his toys and his own little bunk. His bed was a cosy little cupboard where the charts had been stored!

Next we lived in a floathouse, which is a regular house built on a raft of logs. The number one rule on a floathouse is that all children have to wear their lifejackets every time they step out the door. The logs get slimy and slippery and if they fell in between two logs it would be very hard to find the surface again. The children here get used to their lifejackets; sometimes they even forget to take them off when they are in town.

Jarret's school has one room, one teacher and eight students. We don't have a schoolbus, we have a schoolboat. When the class goes ice skating, everyone gets up in the dark and rides on a fishboat for three hours to get to Port McNeill. One day their teacher came in after recess and took the students out to see a pod of dolphins that were nearby. Even the teacher's dog went. When the principal visits, he sometimes arrives in a helicopter. Although many things are different, the school work is the same. Homework must get done and everyone looks forward to weekends.

Jarret and I lived in our floathouse until we asked a neighbour to pull it up onto some land that we bought. The house was very heavy and broke the cable twice. It had to stay half on the beach and half on land for one night and the tide came up inside. The water helped clean up all the broken jam, pickle and salmon jars that had crashed to the floor when the cable broke. The next day it was pulled all the way up. Now we have a garden and Jarret has forts and a treehouse. Our two dogs like it better on land than on the float.

Our community is very small with only about fifty people, but we do have a post office. The mail arrives three times a week by sea plane. When I give my address, people always want to know what street I live on. When I tell them we don't have any streets, they can't believe it and I have to explain that everyone gets around by boat. On Halloween a boat takes all the children trick-or-treating. Another boat brings us propane and gas. One advantage we have is that we never have to wait for a snow plough to clear the roads, although one time there was so much ice on the water that I couldn't get Jarret to the school dock. Sometimes we have to miss things because there is too much wind to go out in the boat, but generally living in an isolated community is a lot of fun.

I am very happy that we decided to stay in Simoom Sound. I think that what I have learned about the whales that pass through here is very important. To learn about a wild animal a scientist has to learn to live near them. Many other people are doing this with chimpanzees, elephants, wolves, lions and other species.

All the plants and animals in an area fit together like a puzzle. If you have only one piece, like a whale in a tank, you really can't see how it fits into the whole picture. This kind of puzzle is called an ecosystem, and it is amazing to see how well everything works together. It is very important to learn as much as possible about ecosystems so that we humans can learn to fit into the puzzle without destroying it. It is my hope that some who read this will go on to study and learn new things about ecosystems that I can read about when I am an old woman. I look forward to that.

This book is about the many things the whales have taught me, and about some of the questions I have not yet found answers to. It is also about just living near whales and trying to fit in.

Severn Cullis-Suzuki
(1979 –)

As a member of Environmental Children's Organization, Severn Cullis-Suzuki, along with her colleagues, raised the funds to attend the 1992 United Nations Conference on Environment and Development in Brazil. There she delivered the following speech to the delegates. The address is reprinted in a book that combines the text with children's drawings of the state of the natural world. In word as well as image, the book tells of the fears of young people for their own futures and the future of nature, but following the advice of her famous dad, the geneticist and environmentalist David Suzuki, she not only talks about but also translates her concern into action.

Tell The World:
A Young Environmentalist Speaks Out
(1993)

Hello, I'm Severn Suzuki speaking on behalf of ECO, the Environmental Children's Organization. We're a group of twelve- and thirteen-year-olds from Canada trying to make a difference. We raised all the money ourselves to come six thousand miles to tell you adults you must change your ways.

Coming up here today, I have no hidden agenda. I am fighting for my future. Losing my future is not like losing an election or a few points on the stock market.

I am here to speak for all future generations. I am here to speak on behalf of the starving children around the world whose cries go unheard. I am here to speak for the countless animals dying across this planet because they have nowhere left to go.

I am afraid to go out in the sun now because of the holes in the ozone. I am afraid to breathe the air because I don't know what chemicals are in it. I used to go fishing in Vancouver with my dad until just a few years ago we found the fish full of cancers. And now we hear about animals and plants becoming extinct every day — vanishing forever.

In my life, I have dreamt of seeing great herds of wild animals, jungles and rainforests full of birds and butterflies, but now I wonder if they will even exist for my children to see. Did you have to worry about these things when you were my age?

All this is happening before our eyes and yet we act as if we have all the time we want and all the solutions. I'm only a child and I don't have all the solutions, but I want you to realize, neither do you!

You don't know how to fix the holes in our ozone layer.

You don't know how to bring salmon back to a dead stream.

You don't know how to bring back an animal now extinct.

And you can't bring back the forests that once grew where there is now a desert.

If you don't know how to fix it, please stop breaking it!

Here you may be delegates of your governments, businesspeople, organizers, reporters or politicians. But really you are mothers and fathers, sisters and brothers, aunts and uncles. And each of you is somebody's child.

I'm only a child, yet I know we are all part of a family, five billion strong — in fact, thirty million species strong — and borders and governments will never change that. I'm only a child, yet I know we are all in this together and should act as one single world toward one single goal. In my anger I am not blind, and in my fear I'm not afraid to tell the world how I feel.

In my country we make so much waste. We buy and throw away, buy and throw away. And yet northern countries will not share with the needy. Even when we have more than enough, we are afraid to lose some of our wealth, afraid to let go.

In Canada, we live a privileged life with plenty of food, water and shelter. We have watches, bicycles, computers and television sets — the list could go on for days.

Two days ago here in Brazil, we were shocked when we spent time with some children living on the streets. And this is what one child told us: "I wish I was rich. And if I were, I would give all the street children food, clothes, medicine, shelter and love and affection." If a child on the street who has nothing is willing to share, why are we who have everything still so greedy?

I can't stop thinking that these children are my own age, and that it makes a tremendous difference where you are born. I could be one of those children living in the favelas of Rio, I could be a child starving in Somalia, a victim of war in the Middle East or a beggar in India.

I'm only a child, yet I know if all the money spent on war was spent on ending poverty and finding environmental answers, what a wonderful place this Earth would be.

At school, even in kindergarten, you teach us how to behave in the world. You teach us:

not to fight with others
to work things out
to respect others
to clean up our mess
not to hurt other creatures
to share, not be greedy

Then why do you go out and do the things you tell us not to do?

Do not forget why you are attending these conferences, who you are doing this for — we are your own children. You are deciding what kind of world we will grow up in.

Parents should be able to comfort their children by saying, "Everything's going to be all right;" "We're doing the best we can" and "It's not the end of the world." But I don't think you can say that to us anymore. Are we even on your list of priorities?

My dad always says, "You are what you do, not what you say."

Well, what you do makes me cry at night.

You grownups say you love us. I challenge you, *please,* make your actions reflect your words.

Thank you for listening.

On the Form

Peri McQuay
(1945 –)

This essay was written as an answer to an article that asserted that nature writing was no longer a legitimate form, since, as a celebration of nature, it obscures the threats facing the natural world.

Seizing the Strawberry
(1994)

Once a man was being chased by a tiger. On and on he raced until he reached a precipice. Frantically, he climbed over the edge; desperately he snatched at a vine. Behind him raged the tiger. Before him was a sheer drop, and, to his horror, at the foot of the cliff he spotted a second tiger, waiting. Just as the man began to realize that the vine was giving way and that there were no available footholds, he saw a luscious red strawberry. Tiger above and tiger below. What did he do? He ate the strawberry.

This Buddhist parable has everything to teach us about living with the despair of seeing nature die. And it is the reason why I am and will continue to be a nature writer. It is right to face the desolation of our time openly and together. Moira Farr's "The Death of Nature Writing" [Brick: *A Literary Journal*, Winter 1993, 16–27] is a courageous statement because in it the author broke through the ring of fear and hopelessness which keeps us from acknowledging that the survival of our world is at stake. However, I strongly disagree with much of what she says.

As a nature writer who continues to be sustained by the writing of her fellows, I have a different understanding of how to face the stake. It was Joanna Macy, in her wise book *World as Lover, World as Self* who reminded me that, even in the face of a final holocaust, sustaining contact with grace is essential. *World as Lover, World as Self* addresses the theme of faith and ecology. Macy acknowledges that "In our collective situation today, with its almost overwhelming social and environmental crises, trusting our own experience means acknowledging our deep, inner responses, our anguish for the world." Although this acknowledgement seems unbearably hard,

Macy believes that by going down into a darkness where there appears to be no faith, we can make redeeming discoveries that "can ground us in our ecology and serve as our faith." Indeed, she believes that our survival depends on our making them. Through the darkness of facing final destruction comes the discovery of what can happen through our agency, or, "as one might express it, grace." Grace "happens when we act with others on behalf of our world." Macy reminds us to take into account the model in nature that living systems evolve in complexity, flexibility, and intelligence through interaction with each other. These interactions require openness and vulnerability in order to process the flow-through of energy and information. They bring into play new responses and new possibilities not previously present, increasing the capacity to effect change. "This interdependent release of fresh potential is called synergy. It is like grace, because it brings an increase of power beyond one's own capacity as a separate entity." As a nature writer, I know that grace happens when a person looks deeply and appreciatively at part of the web and then passes it on.

As a practising nature writer, I'm here to tell you that the reports of my demise are seriously overrated, but first, a small example of synergy at work. I live and work in a conservation area dedicated to giving thousands of children the tools to appreciate their place in nature, tools which they take with them. Children from all areas and backgrounds come, including some who have never set foot in a woods before, and who find the experience frightening. I know this conservation education program works, partly because teachers are astonished by the children's high recall rate, even years after their visits, and also because of the high return rate. The children come back, bringing family and friends, ever widening the circles of appreciation. Of course this example of synergy appears small compared to the power of CEO's to affect change to the land. But as a writer and teacher, I know that all change starts with the self and spreads outwards to others in small ripples. Our greatest act of love and concern is following our path one step at a time, and with all our attentiveness, respect and devotion. Living close to nature, I'm caught in the life-provoking tug of miracles, which I see daily, and also the tonic of a harsh, undeniable reality. Being a writer demands that I stay engaged with both sides.

I've been learning and taking joy from nature writers since my childhood. From my earliest memories, these authors invested me with a sense of wonder — first, pioneer Henri Fabre with his passionate investigation of insects, Ernest Thompson Seton with his canny knowledge of the strange world outside my door, mystical Gene Stratton Porter, then, later, Edwin Way Teale, who evoked intense interest, emotional response, and a feeling of oneness with my surroundings in the out-of-doors. When I read Teale wondering in his conclusion to *A Walk Through the Year* "if the time will ever come when such a book as this will seem like a letter from another world. Will the richness of the natural world be overrun and more and more replaced with a plastic artificial, substitute? The threat is real," and then responding, "the outcome seems to depend on the wisdom and courage and endurance of those who are on the side of life — the original, natural life, the life of the fragile, yet strong, out-of-doors," I was challenged. Always, nature books have been my best companions, teaching me about nature and living, inspiring me, ever provoking me to stay connected to the web of nature. The shelves of my writing room, my sanctuary, are overflowing with John Muir, Henry Beston, Annie Dillard, Gretel Ehrlich, and always, and most of all for me, Loren Eiseley, bone man and poet. It is from these cherished authors that I have learned to honour nature as the sustaining organism of which we are small parts.

Indeed, I can actually say that it was Helen Hoover, her example and her writing, who was my salvation. She set me and my husband on the path which led to our living and writing and teaching in the conservation area. In the late '60s we read and reread *The Gift of the Deer* and *The Longshadowed Forest*. Hoover's story was simple. She and her husband had left well-paying Chicago jobs and moved to a rough cabin in the Minnesota wilds and had survived profound hardships and poverty because living in nature meant so much to them that they could not bear to do otherwise. There was nothing romantic in the story, nothing exotic — the costs of living close to nature were made real. And for the next six years, my husband and I worked our way ever closer to wildness until we found our place in the conservation area where we have lived and worked for the past twenty years.

And now, living in the harsh grace of a hard land, it is my turn to share and interpret my experiences, my vision. Most recently, this has been in the telling of the story of Merak, the human-imprinted red-tailed hawk, who has learned to live in freedom, under our supervision. Letting go, living with risk, living in the moment and appropriate response within the web are all part of what Merak has taught me. Understanding how damaging her fixation with humans has been to her has given me a heightened respect for our need to live in synergy with nature.

It may be that we now must mourn the passing of a way of seeing. Annie Dillard might be one of the last nature writers who could write about nature as if it were a whole. Yet it is Annie Dillard herself who in *Pilgrim at Tinker Creek* warned "There is no guarantee in the world." And Dillard understood very well about eating the strawberry in free fall: "If I am a maple key falling, at least I can twirl." Recognizing our despair over the ravages to the biosystem is necessary. However, when we become paralyzed by despair, we opt out of the organism which is our proper home and become part of the destructive force. This is why I think we need the gift of nature writers' special vision more than ever. Because nature's wholeness is besieged on all sides, affirmative spiritual and philosophical discourse remains essential. It is exactly because we must not take leave of our senses in the face of the holocaust that we need the focus of the visionary.

One concept of what nature writing offers includes "The Great Outdoors. The Unspoiled Wilderness. A place that would always be out there, wild, untouched, free." But surely nature need not be virgin to be venerable. Nature is still the provider of epiphanies. One does not abandon one's mother in her illness. What the death of nature means is that we must live our life as it is given. Prisoners survive their cells by appreciating a square of sky and a spider, by seeing much in little. Indeed, it is in our *natures* to praise, to live fully and to live in hope. Overpreoccupation with disaster leads to paralysis and even death. If we choose life, we might as well live as fully as possible. If we turn from life (which is, after all, nature, which tempers and sustains us) we are dead already.

Nature writing is a two part invention. On the one hand, it is crucial for political writers about ecology, such as David Suzuki to be heard. However, I believe there is an equally important role for the poets of ecology. It is our duty to do whatever we can to stop the CEO of Noranda Mines from mining gold in Yellowstone Park and the host of other assailants *but* we can only do a sustained and effective job of that if first we are very strong in our understanding of who we are and what our place is. This is where the connection with nature offered by nature writers is crucial. According to Zen, life's energy exists in the eye of paradox. And it is indeed paradoxical that we must try to stay in that creative tension, remaining in the duality caused on the one side by our anguish for the destruction of the world, with the unrelenting political action that necessitates, and on the other with our need to eat the strawberries we are offered. Cancer survivors know that we become our thoughts; while we survive, it is our job to sustain that tension, to appreciate, to praise and to operate with hopefulness in the teeth of despair.

I see writing about nature as an attempt to share, rather than to tout, one's exceptional experience. Some of the authors I most admire write about their experiences close to home, for example, Sue Hubbell at her Missouri Ozark farm, and Edwin Way Teale from Trail Wood, his beloved Connecticut acres. The best of nature writers interpret their unique visions of nature, inviting us to see more deeply and with a better understanding. Even in a quiet discourse on the wonder of a bug, they are keeping us in touch with the sacred. I can't accept Farr's "the notion that we are being presented with something new, exotic and unsullied is pure fantasy, and a dangerous one at that." For each of us, life is to some degree another country, unexpected. Each time we stop to look, to really look at a rock, the sparkle, the striations, the weathering, to consider its lifespan of eons, to stroke it, to sense the cold or heat held within it, we are seeing it as new. For that matter, if we are living fully, we are brave and original explorers each moment of our lives. Peter Matthiessen may hang his interior journey on the romantic story of a quest for a snow leopard and Barry Lopez may venture into the arctic's farthest reaches, but these nature writers who travel to exotic places are no different than a child who bends at the waist and peers through his legs to see the world upside down. Moreover, telling one's observations in the form of a vivid story allows the parts to sink deep within us and to work on many levels, long after the book is set aside. Being fallible, nature writers do bring to their investigations preconceived notions, however, usually one of the objects of the exploration is to shed as many of these as possible.

While it is right to point out and analyse fallacies in the North American perception of nature which she thinks fuel fantasy, I have to say that I do not think nature writers are the ones guilty of disseminating these misinterpretations. For example, I cannot recall any of the dozens of nature writers from the 1800s to the present whom I have read who have not presented nature as savage in tooth and claw. Surely Walt Disney's perpetrations should not be held against us.

As for the wretchedly common fallacy that "Nature isn't us," that we can somehow maintain life outside of the biospheric web, I have to answer that the many nature authors I read reiterate that we are nature and nature is us. For example, one of my first teachers was pioneer ecologist John H. Storer, who, in 1956 in his popular book *The Web of Life*, was celebrating "the teamwork and delicate balance existing between the different forces that keep life functioning on this planet." He concluded *The Web of Life* by warning, "Destroy it [the land] and man is destroyed." In his preface to Francis Fukuoka's revolutionary *The One Straw Revolution*, in 1978, Wendell Berry was writing "Mr. Fukuoka has understood that we cannot isolate one aspect of life from another."

While it is true that there is a "wide gulf between the worlds of science and literature" which has led to the excessively academic bent of science, I believe that it is here, as mediators between the two aspects, that nature writers have always excelled. As Stephen Trimble writes in his introduction to his anthology *Words From the Land*, "In seeing nature as a teacher, and yourself not as an expert but as a listener, naturalists part company from scientists." Moreover, Trimble notes, "in integrating science with art, and still retaining her capacity for innocence, Carson manages to do what Barry Lopez also aims for as a goal. He says that a writer must try 'to cultivate a sense of yourself as one who doesn't know. As long as you do this, you don't run the risk of writing the story as though you were the expert. The authority will always be with the subject.'" Trimble continues, "naturalist writers thrive on such juxtapositions, on a mix of experience and knowledge, adventure and contemplation, humanism and science. Robert Finch calls it 'reintegrating the disciplines.'"

Protesting the emphasis on the white male worldview which is absorbed when we read predominantly male authors, Farr objects, for example, to the "gruff, Marlboro Man-ish quality to many of the writings of Edward Abbey or Peter Matthiessen." They swagger a bit, she says, "as though trying to woo through impressive, virile achievement." And she further objects to their machismo posturing. Now "machismo" is defined as "the need to prove one's virility by courage or daring." But I think it is important to be careful to distinguish experimenting with risk and a self-seeking proving in risky situations. I find Peter Matthiessen's accounts of his practise of Zen in wilderness generous-spirited and very far from swaggering. Matthiessen himself explains that his adventures place him where danger is a constant reality and he says he likes this because the penalty for error helps keep him in the Zen state of mindfulness. Gary Nabhan, author of the prize-winning book *Gathering the Desert*, says Matthiessen is someone who shows "Incredible growth as a human being and as a writer, taking risks all over," someone who moves natural history writing beyond its "one little clustered set of styles and ideas."

Nature writing as a discipline has inspired some of the most elegant and compressed writing (Barry Lopez and Loren Eiseley for two examples), and it also has produced the rough unevenness of an Edward Abbey. Abbey, in his careless and jocular tone, may seem bent on hiding the feeling quality of his modern-day assessment of Thoreau but anyone who could read "Down the River With Henry David Thoreau" and not emerge with a renewed zest for Thoreau in his earthiness and his reverence is missing the skill with which the trail of quotes is laid down. I may not admire Abbey's particular brand of swashbuckling adventure, but I would not want to miss his salty perceptions.

Place beside the cerebral and the adventurous the lyrical. I think of Richard Nelson's celebration of the mystery and complexity of life, *The Island Within*, written by a cultural anthropologist who had spent twenty-five years studying the relationship between native peoples and their environments.

Nature writing logically focuses on experiences in nature. However, because nearly all of us authors come in and out of nature in our lives, we are fitted as interpreters to help bridge the gap between nature and those who live their lives on almost purely human terms.

Although I find it indefensible that previously the voices of women experiencing nature were largely denied us, I glory in the many examples of women writing of nature before the seventies which are included in the magnificent anthology *Sisters of the Earth*, among them Theodora Stanwell-

Fletcher's radiant account of Christmas in an unexplored wilderness in north-central British Columbia, isolated from neighbours and experiencing dangerous cold.

Furthermore, speaking as a woman nature writer myself, and also as a woman who grew up reading predominantly male nature authors, I have to agree with Ann Zwinger: "I've never gone into nature as a woman; I've gone as a person. I'm not sure but what in other guises men and women perceive the landscape very differently. But I think as nature writers you have a focus, and you have a discipline, and that is a very precise one — to find out what's going on — and you put aside all feelings of femininity or masculinity. I don't see it as a sex difference. I just see it as a bent of personality." I delight in Virginia Woolf's idea that a poet or novelist should express both the male and female mind, that both exist inside each one of us and that the poles should come together in creation. Woolf believed that "when the fusion of male and female takes place that mind is fully fertilised and uses all its faculties." It is this fertile ground which inspires the nature writing I have prized. Where the differentiation in sex is significant is in its inspirational value: "If other women can do this, so can I."

And my own position as a nature writer? Joanna Macy says "action on behalf of life transforms." What is needed is to allow room for both the political and the spiritual in nature writing. I have always seen it as my challenge not to preach but to invite readers inside my home, the web, indeed to make it so alluring and plausible that this web is home, that they will care for it and act on its behalf. Barry Lopez says of his writing, "Your work is your prayer." What interests me most, and what is enduring in the best of nature writing is the sacred. The web is broken in many places, perhaps critically, but in this "now" where we must live, the strands themselves glisten with beauty and meaning.

Ann Zwinger tells of a dream she had of nuclear holocaust "somewhere off the edge, off the horizon." While she waited for the disaster to reach her, she sat doing what mattered most, writing "words that would remain hanging in the dry desert air, suspended with a life of their own, witnesses to grace and coherence. That was all that mattered."

"The words."

You take Annie Dillard's "huge steps, trying to feel the planet's roundness arc between your feet" and you take small, hesitant ones, feeling for the grains of former mountains under your soles. You bear witness. Always, you bear witness. You fumble toward Joanna Macy's magnificent synergy, trying to touch people, to make those connections that create more than the sum of their parts. But, through sorrow, horror and some-time despair, you do walk on and you do eat the strawberry.

Permissions

"Chapter 10" from *I Married the Klondike* by Laura Berton. Copyright 1954 and 1961 by Laura Beatrice Berton and Pierre Berton. Reprinted by permission of McClelland and Stewart Limited.

"The Subtlety of Land" from *Perfection of the Morning* by Sharon Butala. Copyright 1994 by Sharon Butala. Reprinted by permission of HarperCollins Publishers Ltd.

"Green" from *Growing Pains: The Autobiography of Emily Carr* by Emily Carr. Copyright 1946. Reprinted by permission of Stoddart Publishing/Irwin Publishing.

"White Currants" and "Beginnings" from *The Book of Small* by Emily Carr. Copyright 1942. Reprinted by permission of Stoddart Publishing/Irwin Publishing.

"How the World Began" from *Life Lived Like a Story: Life Stories of Three Yukon Native Elders* edited by Julie Cruikshank. Copyright 1990 by the University of Nebraska Press. Reprinted by permission of University of Nebraska Press.

Tell the World: A Young Environmentalist Speaks Out by Severn Cullis-Suzuki. Copyright 1993 by Severn Cullis-Suzuki. Reprinted by permission of Doubleday Canada Limited.

"Chapters 12 and 13" from *Cabin at Singing River: Building a Home in the Wilderness* by Chris Czajkowski. Copyright 1991 by Chris Czajkowski. Reprinted by permission of Camden House.

"Merry Christmas to All" from *River for My Sidewalk* by Gilean Douglas. Copyright 1991 by Gilean Douglas. Reprinted by permission of Sono Nis press.

"The Lost Salmon Run" and "The Grey Archway" from *Legends of Vancouver* by E. Pauline Johnson-Tekahionwake. Copyright 1991. Reprinted by permission of Quarry Press, Inc.

Further Reading

Anderson, Lorraine (ed). 1991. *Sisters of the Earth: Women's Prose and Poetry about Nature.* New York: Vintage Books, a Division of Random House.

Bennett, Jennifer. 1991. *Lilies of the Hearth: The Historical Relationship Between Women and Plants.* Camden East: Camden House.

_____ . 1994. *Our Gardens Ourselves: Reflections of an Ancient Art.* Camden East. Camden House.

Breen, Neeaham Howard, Sandy Frances Duncan, Deborah Ferens, Phyllis Reeve, Susan Yates (eds). 1994. *Witness to Wilderness: The Clayoquot Sound Anthology.* Vancouver: Arsenal Pulp Press.

Corrigan, Theresa and Stephanie Hoppe (eds). 1989. *With a Fly's Eye, Whale's Wit, and Woman's Heart: Animals and Women.* San Francisco: Cleis Press.

Diamond, Irene and Gloria Feman Orenstein (eds). 1990. *Reweaving the World: The Emergence of Ecofeminism.* San Francisco: Sierra Club Books.

Finch, Robert and John Elder (eds). 1990. *The Norton Book of Nature Writing.* New York: W.W. Norton & Company.

Frye, Northrop. 1971. *The Bush Garden: Essays on the Canadian Imagination.* Toronto: Anansi.

Grady, Wayne (ed). 1991. *From the Country: Writings About Rural Canada.* Camden East: Camden House.

Grady, Wayne (ed). 1992. *Treasures of Place: Three Centuries of Nature Writing in Canada.* Vancouver: Douglas & McIntyre.

Knowles, Karen (ed). 1992. *Celebrating the Land: Women's Nature Writings, 1850 – 1991*. Flagstaff, Arizona: Northland Publishing.

Mabey, Richard (ed). 1995. *The Oxford Book of Nature Writing*. Oxford: Oxford University Press.

Mies, Maria and Vandana Shiva (eds). 1993. *Ecofeminism*. Halifax: Fernwood Publications.

Moses, Daniel David and Terry Goldie (eds). 1992. *An Anthology of Canadian Native Literature in English*. Toronto: Oxford University Press.

Norwood, Vera. 1993. *Made from the Earth: American Women and Nature*. Chapel Hill: North Carolina Press.

Plant, Judith (ed). 1989. *Healing the Wounds: The Promise of Ecofeminism*. Toronto: Between the Lines.

_____ and Christopher Plant (eds). 1990. *Turtle Talk: Voices for a Sustainable Future*. Lillooet, BC: New Society Publishers.

Tippett, Maria. 1992. *By a Lady: Celebrating Three Centuries of Art by Canadian Women*. Toronto: Penguin.

Von Baeyer, Edwinna and Pleasance Crawford (eds). 1995. *Garden Voices: Two Centuries of Canadian Garden Writing*. Toronto: Random House of Canada.